AF269648

TIMES REMEMBERED

The Final Years of the Bill Evans Trio

by
Joe La Barbera and Charles Levin

Number 15 in the North Texas Lives
of Musicians Series

University of North Texas Press
Denton, Texas

©2021 Joe La Barbera and Charles Levin
Foreword ©2021 Harold Miller
All rights reserved.
Printed in the United States of America.

10 9 8 7 6 5 4 3 2

Permissions:
University of North Texas Press
1155 Union Circle #311336
Denton, TX 76203-5017

The paper used in this book meets the minimum requirements of the American National Standard for Permanence of Paper for Printed Library Materials, z39.48.1984. Binding materials have been chosen for durability.

Library of Congress Cataloging-in-Publication Data

La Barbera, Joe, 1948– author. | Levin, Charles (Writer on music), 1951– author. | Miller, Hal, 1941– writer of foreword.
Times remembered: the final years of the Bill Evans Trio / Joe La Barbera and Charles Levin.
Pages cm
Includes bibliographical references and index.
ISBN-13 978-1-57441-844-6 (cloth)
ISBN-13 978-1-57441-854-5 (ebook)
1. Bill Evans Trio. 2. Evans, Bill, 1929–1980—Last years. 3. La Barbera, Joe. 4. Johnson, Marc, 1953–. 5. Jazz musicians—United States—Biography. 6. Jazz—1971–1980—History and criticism. 7. BISAC: MUSIC / Genres & Styles / Jazz. 8. MUSIC / Individual Composer & Musician. 9. LCGFT: Biographies.

ML421.B5447 L3 2021
781.65092/2 [B]–dc23
2021023734

Number 15 in the North Texas Lives of Musicians Series

The electronic edition of this book was made possible by the support of the Vick Family Foundation. Typeset by vPrompt eServices.

This book is dedicated to the memory
of William John Evans
(August 16, 1929–September 15, 1980)

"I follow my code and am at peace with myself."

—Bill Evans

Contents

Foreword

I t was 1962 and the Bill Evans Trio with Paul Motian and Chuck Israels was playing a club in New York City—I think it was Café Bohemia. By this time, Bill had already completed his historic stay with the Miles Davis Sextet (*Jazz Track, Kind of Blue*) and his all-too brief time with his super-innovative trio with bassist Scott LaFaro and drummer Paul Motian (*Portrait in Jazz, Sunday at the Village Vanguard*), so not surprisingly the club was noisy, buzzing with that preperformance din we know so well as the seats began to fill.

And, then, like magic, Bill began to play—I think it was "Everything Happens to Me" and the quiet that quickly materialized became part reverence, part awe, part wonder and, no doubt, part gratitude. Anyone who's ever heard the Bill Evans Trio live is totally familiar with this phenomenon. Call it the *Bill Evans effect*, if you will. Bill Evans was in the house.

So much has been written about Bill Evans throughout his career and ever since his death in 1980. Had Evans accomplished nothing else other than his contribution to *Kind of Blue* or his genre-changing trio-recording of *Live at the Village Vanguard*, he would still be a jazz household name, and a musical influence on countless other pianists around the world. But today, here in 2020, some forty years since his untimely death at age 51, Evans continues to be the subject of innumerable books, magazine articles and past interviews, all seeking to explain and explore this pianist whose piano and composing mastery now constitute a veritable *Bill Evans School of Playing*. To be fair, considerable information about Bill Evans has been amassed as a result of these myriad sources and, of course, there are the recordings which now number in the hundreds given the numerous bootlegs. And there are the countless Bill Evans photos, virtually each one of which shows him in his characteristic serious mien or seemingly as part of the piano itself.

Forty years gone. It hardly seems possible.

Though he left us all too soon and unprepared for the artistic void which followed in his wake, Bill Evans bestowed a legacy of recordings that sets him apart from just about any other pianist in the history of jazz. Although he was a prominent figure during what could be termed as a *Golden Age of Jazz Piano*, as represented by Thelonious Monk, Chick Corea, Herbie Hancock, Keith Jarrett, Marian McPartland, Ahmad Jamal, McCoy Tyner, Oscar Peterson, Dave Brubeck and others as well, Bill Evans continues to stand out as a unique original, sounding like no one else and an enduring model and inspiration to so many others, including some of these afore-mentioned peers.

Perhaps more so than any other jazz pianist of the past half century, Bill Evans could make any kind of song—however unlikely—a *Bill Evans song* or so it seemed. He didn't compose many of his repertoire staples, such as "Nardis," "Theme From MASH," "Someday My Prince Will Come," "Emily" and "My Foolish Heart" and a number of others. But their identity with the pianist is so indelible that we think of those songs as Bill Evans songs.

Similarly, Bill Evans—*the composer*—is well represented in the annals of jazz with "Waltz for Debby, "Re: Person I Knew," "Turn Out The Stars," "Blue in Green," "Peace Piece," "Time Remembered," and more but yet, when others plays these songs, it is Evans who almost always come to mind.

Few other musicians have enjoyed the unanimity of approval that is attached to Bill Evans around the world; yet, relatively little is known about this enigmatic composer/improviser who reminded us all of the intrinsic beauty of the waltz, whose approach to accompaniment and improvisation produced ballads of supreme poignancy as well as technical mastery and whose trios had their own special kind of swing magic. One wonders whether the term *modal music* would have ever acquired its present cache and preeminence had it not been for Evans' playing on *Kind of Blue* and *Jazz Track*. Just try and imagine the state of jazz had there been no Bill Evans.

Although Bill Evans was undoubtedly one of the most articulate jazz musicians ever, all the questions still persist—*who was Bill Evans?*

Times Remembered: The Final Years of the Bill Evans Trio, written by Bill's last trio drummer, Joe La Barbera and co-author Charles Levin, attempts to further answer those questions. Given La Barbera's close relationship with Evans throughout the two years of the trio's existence, *Times Remembered* presents the reader with a veritable gold mine of information about its subject. This book draws a number of parallels between La Barbara's family and career and that of Evans if only to highlight the near-inevitability of their joining forces musically at some point. Both were greatly influenced and encouraged by older siblings: in Bill's case, his brother Harry, a pianist and music educator; in Joe's case, his multi-instrumentalist father, saxophonist brother Pat and trumpeter-arranger brother John. Evans and the La Barbera brothers all came from first-generation immigrant families who accorded music a special place in their lives and fell in love with the music called jazz early in their lives.

The fact that Joe spent copious amounts of personal time with Bill Evans throughout their two-year relationship provided him a view and perspective denied most other Evans chroniclers and observers, and that gave him a vantage point from which much of the book was constructed. Joe was often more of a roommate and friend than just a musical peer. Theirs was a close relationship made all the more difficult and challenging because of Bill's personal foibles.

This story of Bill Evans does not purport to be a Bill Evans bio. It is an up-close look at one of the towering musical figures of the 20th century over a two-year period, the last two of his life, with his remarkably superb trio consisting of La Barbera and bassist Marc Johnson, which produced some of the finest music of his career. It is a story of a friend and colleague who knew him well and who fully recognized that this story was drawing to a close.

Whether there are lessons to be learned or conclusions to be drawn from an examination of Bill Evans' life is something for others to ponder and reflect upon. What cannot be disputed, however, and what this book proclaims loud and clear, is that Bill Evans was a musical genius who, notwithstanding formidable obstacles and challenges, established himself as one of the most significant creative artists of his time and beyond. Like that small pantheon of jazz immortals, such as Louis Armstrong, Art Tatum, Charlie Parker, Duke Ellington, Miles Davis, John Coltrane and few others, Bill Evans was one of the supreme creative architects of this music who changed it forever.

Hal Miller
Albany, NY
June 8, 2020

Acknowledgments

What began as an email from Joe to Charles in May 2012—*Can you help me write a book about Bill Evans?*—is now a reality. But getting there—translating and verifying memories of times lived more than 40 years ago—was no easy task. Many friends and professionals selflessly helped us reach this goal. Like in many works of this nature, not everyone's contribution found its way onto these pages. But we thank you all for whatever information, small or large, that you offered us.

The authors want to thank Karen DeVinney, former managing editor at University of North Texas Press, for her enthusiastic response to our proposal. And kind thanks to Ron Chrisman, UNT Press' director, who took over the project after Karen retired. Ron, we appreciate your steady hand and especially your patience.

Our book relied on witness statements from numerous folks in the orbit of Bill Evans' and Joe's lives. These comments loaned a sense of place and veracity to this story. Thanks to John Di Martino, Alphonso Johnson, Marc Johnson, Laurie Verchomin, Malcolm Page, Tunde Agbi, Garry Dial, Gary Novak, Marc Copland, Jon Mayer, Tiffany La Barbera-Palmer, Andy LaVerne, Denny Zeitlin, Peter Erskine, Richie Beirach and Adam Nussbaum.

Thanks to Eddie Arkin, Bevan Manson, John La Barbera, Pat La Barbera, Jimi Fox, Richard Scheinin, Dan DiPiero and John Steinmetz—trusted friends—who read our work at various stages, some in spare chapters, others in full drafts. Your comments and feedback gave us much to chew on, revise (in some cases) and celebrate. More importantly, it assured us that the reader was hearing Joe's voice in telling this story. A big shout

out to Harold "Hal" Miller, long time La Barbera family friend, jazz drummer, jazz historian, and former associate director for the New York State Division of Youth mentoring hundreds of at-risk youths. Hal gave the initial submission to UNT Press a good looking over and with that came lots of excellent suggestions. We also want to extend our deep thanks to Hal for the wonderful Foreword he wrote for this book.

Likewise, we are immensely grateful to Bruce Klauber and Chris Smith, UNT Press's chosen peer reviewers, who greeted our manuscript with enthusiasm, praise and thoughtful critique. We are also deeply indebted to our indexer, Cameron Kiszla, and Ken Maryanski for last-minute assists with editing. Also, thanks to Raymond Fox, a true *Photoshop Yoda*, who made old photos look fresh and new again.

Thanks also to Rosa Mazon and Ljiljana Grubisic at the Los Angeles Philharmonic Archives; Tim Jackson at Monterey Jazz Festival and Kuumbwa Jazz Center; Bennett Jackson at Kuumbwa Jazz Center; Sarah Weller at Ronnie Scott's Jazz Club; Tonya Weber at Iowa Public Television; Samuel Hyde, Nicholas Heyd and Abigail Simmons at the Bill Evans Archive, Southeastern Louisiana University; Deborah Ross at George Wein Festival Productions; Leon Terjanian; Steve Hillis; Michael Bloom; Jimmy Bralower; Darlene Craviotto; Jordan Fox; and Ted Panken.

A big special thank you to Tonino Vantaggiato, whose training as a jazz and classical bassist combined with an historian's endless curiosity, supplied us with an exhaustive work documenting Bill Evans' performances (Thank you, Laurie Verchomin, for the recommendation!). And the same gratitude to François Lacharme for his moving and poetic essay, *Sorrow in Soho*, and the wonderful photos he unearthed from the L'Espace Cardin concerts. Both of their contributions were significant in telling this story.

Joe La Barbera would like to personally thank his family for always being there in every way. To my one and only Gillian, Tiffany, Eric and, of course, my brothers, I am eternally grateful to pass through this life with your love and mine for each of you.

In writing this book, eventually, I realized that to do justice to Bill, I needed to get help from an actual writer. Fortunately I knew the person I wanted, former student and now colleague and dear friend Charles Levin.

We were both encouraged as people from around the globe began contributing to and confirming what I had remembered.

Charles Levin would like to thank Joe La Barbera, the man who invented optimism and showed me more patience as a drum student than could be imagined. Thanks for giving me the opportunity to share this story about you and Bill with the world. I also want to thank Jimi Fox, my closest friend of 40-plus years. The Prologue of this book benefited from your sharp read. On to Cuba soon, my friend! My biggest heartfelt thanks and unconditional love to my partner, Jeni Breen. I know you have my back as I have yours. I'm so glad we reconnected.

Introduction

In January 1980, I joined Bill Evans' trio in New York. The experiences of the next 20 months, musical and otherwise, would leave an indelible imprint on me, which remains to this day. Initially, I started to write down things as they popped into my head, which they did with great frequency for the first 20 years after Bill's death. It became a therapeutic and obsessive endeavor.

What you are about to read is factual and written with love and respect.

—Joe La Barbera

Prologue

Bill's girlfriend Laurie hopped into the back seat with the $150 he owed me. We'd stopped at Helen Keane's—Bill's longtime manager and producer—to get the money. We came into town only because Bill finally agreed to see his doctor, his health hanging by what now seemed like a thread. Laurie and I had implored Bill for weeks to see a physician, but he'd refused, instead self-medicating with his preferred daily regimen. We'd started a trio gig at Fat Tuesday's a week earlier but Bill, his body crashing, lasted just two nights.

Just as we were ready to head home, a horrendous groan erupted from the back seat. I wheeled around to see Bill coughing up blood. My pulse jumped. I'm not cool under fire, but I instinctively knew this was a life-or-death situation. Bill knew it too. *Get me to the nearest emergency room. Mount Sinai ...*

I was parked heading east on 98th Street. Mt. Sinai Hospital was behind us to the west on Madison Avenue. I made my way toward Park Avenue and hung a left, then left again on the first street I could turn onto. It was one-way, and I was going the wrong direction. Bill told me to lay on the horn. *Tell them it's an emergency.* I hollered at drivers in the snarl of car exhaust that was midday Manhattan. Finally, another left on Madison Avenue and, once again, driving against traffic. More hollering, more laying on the horn, but still the quickest route to the emergency room.

We pulled into the ambulance bay, and I half carried, half walked Bill out of the car. Laurie recited Bill's medical history to the triage nurse (including his drug abuse) as I took him to a treatment room. A nurse told me to wait outside.

Chapter 1

A Child is Born
1904–1966

Shortly after my father was born in 1904, an itinerant fortune teller wandered into Cerda, the 14th-century village where his family lived in Sicily. An elderly man, the soothsayer fielded a small tray filled with pieces of paper. Each paper held a prediction. A parrot sat on the man's shoulder and for the equivalent of a penny, the bird reached down and plucked one of the papers. My grandmother, Salvatrice La Barbera, asked to know about her newborn's lot in life. The paper read, "Your son is going to be a musician." Salvatrice panicked. Musicians can't make a living, she reasoned. Music is as central to Italian life as wine or pasta but it was a difficult if not impossible existence as a professional. Singing for your supper was not just a catchy phrase but a reality. Besides, she'd already set her sights on a more prosperous and stable life in America.

Italy in those days operated under the feudal system. Peasants like my grandparents could not own land; only the privileged class could. The best they could hope for was leasing a plot and paying for it in cash or crops. Land was scarce and very difficult to come by.

As a child, my grandpa, Pasquale, worked as a "caruso"—an indentured servant—for the local baron. He spent his days—from pre-dawn to late evening—standing chest high in the irrigation ditches, paddling freezing water through irrigation canals with his bare arms, hands and body, so it reached the crops. The work was hard. Early human rights activist Booker T. Washington describes the horror of these conditions in his book *The Man Farthest Down: A Record of Observation and Study in Europe.*

During this time, my grandpa befriended the baron's children. They were close in age and often played together on Sundays after mass. My grandfather had attended three years of school before being indentured, so he could read and write and taught these skills to the baron's two kids. Not being literate himself, the baron was astonished and pleased, so upon releasing my grandpa from servitude at age 17, he rewarded him with a plot of land to sharecrop. By the time my father, Joseph, came along, my grandparents farmed the land, owned a goat and mule and had a small house in the village. Then my grandfather's health deteriorated. The work as a child in the irrigation ditches had taken a toll on him, and he was unable to work the land. Debts came due, so my grandparents sold the mule and a cart as well as other possessions.

Meanwhile, my grandpa's brother, Salvatore, had offered tickets for passage to America. Until now, my grandfather refused them out of pride and a sense of being successful in Italy. But my grandmother, Salvatrice, was an incredibly strong and determined woman. Unfortunately, my only memories of her are tainted with fear because by the time I came along, she'd developed severe dementia while living with our family. In the end, she was the one who decided on moving to America, with or without her husband. Finally, he relented, and in 1911, my grandmother, father, his older sister, Giuseppa, and younger brother Salvatore set sail from mainland Italy for Ellis Island in New York. They were leaving poverty for a chance at prosperity.

My father would often recount the story of that trip, sailing across the Atlantic in the worst storm to date. Like others of their class, they traveled in steerage, a large open space, deep below decks, with hammocks strung along the side of the ship. The storm rocked the boat back and forth. A plate of spaghetti would slide away from pop while he ate and then just as quickly slide back toward him; he found this funny. Above deck, it was no laughing matter. The waves reached such heights that the crew covered the air intakes

The La Barbera family in Sicily photographed in 1911 as a keepsake prior
to sailing to America. This type of photo was commonplace in the event the
family might be lost at sea, which nearly happened in this case. L-R, Josephine
La Barbera, Salvatrice La Barbera, Salvatore La Barbera, Pasquale La Barbera.
Holding hoop is Joseph La Barbera (Joe's dad). *Photo courtesy of Joe La Barbera.*

lest people drown below. Three seamen perished during this storm. The ship
was blown so far off course, it landed in Nova Scotia and then made its
way down to Manhattan. (Many years later, my older brother John would
find a story inside the *New York Times*, corroborating my father's account
in detail. In a two-column feature dated November 11, 1911, the ship's

captain described their crossing as "the worst weather I have encountered in 24 years at sea.")[1]

The family cleared the authorities at Ellis Island and then stayed in New York City for a few nights. Their destination was Mt. Morris, a small town in western New York about an hour south of Rochester and an hour east of Buffalo. My grandfather's brother, Salvatore (who had provided the tickets), lived there and helped them get settled. My grandfather had stayed behind. He'd developed emphysema from the years of hard child labor. In those days, if you showed up at Ellis Island with a cough, the authorities quarantined you or, worse yet, sent you home. So a year later, the family pooled their money and bought him a first-class passage, which entitled him to walk into America, no questions asked.

My grandparents bought a house on the outskirts of town. As luck would have it, the property sat on a natural gravel pit that the village needed for building a road, so my grandparents sold it for a profit. With that money, they bought a larger lot in 1927 and built a new home at 100 Stanley Street. It cost about $2,000 to construct the two-story, three-bedroom, two-bath house—large by the day's standards. (By then, my father was about 18 and working, so the money he earned helped pay for it.) The property had three lots on it. The idea was that someday the grandkids would build a home there. Our parents' hopes were dashed however, because like most kids—especially those interested in music—we had to leave or there would have been no future in it.

When my grandfather arrived in America, he was literate. He'd write and translate letters for anyone in the community who needed his help. But a few years after arriving, his health failed and, in 1915, he passed away. He was 45 years old. When he died, my grandmother could not easily support the family. A local priest arranged for my father and his younger brother to live at Father Baker's Home for Boys, a nationally known orphanage in a Buffalo suburb. While this eased my grandmother's financial burden, she hoped the school would instill in them a respect for authority. While living there, my father learned to sew, bake and play music, starting with piccolo and baritone horn (instruments typical of a New Orleans brass band which—no small coincidence—were modeled on Sicilian street bands).

When my father turned 14, my grandmother pulled him out of the orphanage because it was now necessary for him to get a job and help support the family. An uncle got him a job on the railroad as a water boy. But now my grandmother was pleased that he was leaving. He'd learned to speak Polish there (the predominant immigrant population of the city and orphanage), and she fretted that he'd become more fluent at that language than Italian. For the next 20 years, my father worked on the railroad.

Meanwhile, his passion for music grew every day. He began collecting and learning to play instruments, starting with clarinet and gradually adding valve trombone and other brass. He'd practice in the caboose. By the time he was 20, he played in concert and dance bands around Mt. Morris. By 30, he began leading his own ensembles and directing the American Legion band. Except for the lessons he got at the orphanage, he was a completely self-taught musician.

At 36, my father took a job with the New York State Civil Service as a stationary engineer. To do this, he enrolled in a home-study course to earn an engineering diploma—all by a man with a fifth-grade education. He took a job in the power plant of Mt. Morris Tuberculosis Hospital, where my mother, Josephine Cipolla, would eventually work as a nurse. They married on June 26, 1943 and remained a loving and happy couple forevermore. Unlike my grandfather who sported a moustache (fashionable in his day), my father was clean-shaven. And while my grandmother wore her hair up (also the look back then), my mom wore hers to the neckline. I'm biased, of course, but my folks were two of the sweetest people you'd ever meet. They were always smiling (unless I was driving them crazy).

My oldest brother, Pascel "Pat" Emmanuel La Barbera, was born on April 7, 1944. John Phillip La Barbera arrived on November 10, 1945. When each was about 5, my father laid out a bunch of instruments on the living room sofa and asked them to choose. Pat picked the violin and, after one lesson, switched to clarinet. John chose the cornet (also from the Sicilian marching band) which he played until high school when he switched to trumpet. I was born on February 22, 1948. Not quite the same ritual for me. My father showed me a drum set because he needed a drummer for his master plan—a family band. After many years as a local bandleader, my father was

Joseph La Barbera (Joe's dad), c. 1933, in a publicity photo for his job as a local bandleader. Pop led bands of all styles and sizes. He once played opposite Earl "Fatha" Hines at a local roadhouse called Fisher's Fun Farm. *Photo courtesy of Joe La Barbera.*

determined to lead a group that he had full control over. A year later, I also took up clarinet and saxophone, which I played through high school.

By 5, I was playing gigs with my father and brothers. But soon my mother decided she wanted in after spending a Saturday night home alone while we played a gig. So my father taught her to play the bass. He drew a fingering chart, which showed where to place her left hand on the bass' fingerboard to produce the correct notes. She put the chart on the wall over the sink and studied it while washing dishes after meals. She never dropped a dish—or a beat! In fact, my brothers and I would press her into service for our jam sessions if the regular player couldn't make it. That she did this was not surprising. My mother's generation was raised to believe that young girls got jobs to help support the family and eventually marry, have children and stay at home. But Josephine Cipolla (Italian for onion) had another vision for how her life would play out. In 1928, New York State opened a new program in nurses training at The Craig Colony for Epileptics in neighboring Sonyea (State of New York Epileptic Asylum). Back then, young women who weren't under constant supervision by their families were looked down upon in shame. Nevertheless, my mother was determined and enrolled, paving the way for her four younger siblings to follow. All became medical professionals.

By 1955 (the same year that Bill Evans moved to New York), the La Barbera Family Band was intact. We played weddings, banquets and retirement and anniversary parties—whatever was required. Our setlist was a smorgasbord of styles: Italian polkas and mazurkas; popular songs of the day from Perry Como, Tony Bennett and Rosemary Clooney (I was singing back then!); and swing-era, big band, jazz hits from Count Basie, Duke Ellington, Glenn Miller, Fletcher Henderson and Artie Shaw. John played cornet, Pat was on alto sax and clarinet, my father on piano, mother on bass and myself on drums—just like a New Orleans jazz band.

Most of the music my brothers and I heard was on recordings. Most venues offering live shows (so we thought) were an hour's drive north in Rochester. Some of those venues would not allow minors. However, in Mt. Morris, where we lived, one club featured weekly live jazz shows—the LaDelfa Hotel. This establishment was owned and operated by the family of a man I would befriend when I was 15, Bob LaDelfa. Bob was a good drummer and mentor who would take my brothers and me to hear live jazz in Rochester or Buffalo. Artists like Terry Gibbs; the Soft Winds with Herb Ellis, Johnny Frigo and Ray Brown; and swing drumming legend Gene Krupa all performed in Mt. Morris. My father once took me to a

La Barbera Family Band in a publicity shot, c. 1955. Taken about the time that the band auditioned in Rochester for a spot on the Mickey Mouse Club television show. L-R, Joseph La Barbera, Pat La Barbera, Joe La Barbera, Josephine La Barbera, John La Barbera. *Photo courtesy of Joe La Barbera.*

matinee and hoisted me on his shoulders for about five minutes to hear this great drummer. With Krupa was Dave McKenna on piano and Eddie Shu on tenor saxophone.

Our family band also entered a few talent shows, including Ted Mack's Original Amateur Hour, where we met and shared an ice cream cone with Mr. Mack. We also auditioned for the Mickey Mouse Club television program during a nationwide talent search that stopped in Rochester. The audition was held on the top floor of Sibley's, a large, local department store. We made it to the finals that day but lost out to a youngster named Steve Gadd, who not only played drums but tap danced too. Steve and I would cross paths several times in later years.

At school, every kid wanted to play drums, but the clarinet seat was vacant, so I got drafted. I also played some tenor sax in the school's dance band (the term "jazz band" was forbidden back then). Meanwhile, I was learning swing-era drumming for my father's music and digesting earlier drummers like Baby Dodds. Thanks, indirectly, to the school's hip band director, I was starting to devour bebop drumming as well.

His name was Frank Matina, a large, youngish guy, probably in his late 20s or early 30s, who played bass (in my junior and senior year, I would play gigs with him). Unlike his predecessor, he wasn't an "old school" musician, who was primarily interested in concert band and marching band music. Mr. Matina embraced bebop's upstart, modern sounds. Using the band-class budget, he signed up with the Columbia Record Club, a popular, mail-order service that gave you deals on brand new LPs. He let brother Pat pick the records, which turned out to be a game changer for me and my brothers. We owe a large debt to Frank Matina for his guidance, encouragement and patience.

In those days, my parents had introduced us to Count Basie, Benny Goodman and Glenn Miller, whose music we loved and performed at gigs. We pored over these sounds on the family's tiny stereo—a portable, red unit with detachable speakers that played 33⅓ vinyl LP records and smaller 45 RPM singles, the latter with a plastic spacer inserted in the disk's large hole. The stereo, a meager 1½ watts of power, traveled between our basement—where I practiced with my brothers and parents—and the kitchen—where we constantly listened to music during meals. Primitive by today's standards, but enough technology to change my life.

Meanwhile, Pat often brought home modern sounds, courtesy of Mr. Matina and the record club—artists whose style really grabbed us. In time, we discovered Lester Young, Charlie Parker and Dizzy Gillespie. One day in late 1959, Pat walked in with a Miles Davis LP called, *Jazz Track*. Recorded a year earlier, it was Miles' first studio takes of "On Green Dolphin Street," "Stella by Starlight" and "Put Your Little Foot Right Out" (also called "Fran Dance"). For this session, Miles used the same ensemble that would later record his landmark classic, *Kind of Blue*: Cannonball Adderley on alto sax; John Coltrane, tenor sax; Bill Evans, piano; Paul Chambers, bass; and Jimmy Cobb, drums. (The A-side featured tracks that Miles recorded with a European band that included expatriate Kenny Clarke on drums for a French film soundtrack.)[2] Until that moment, the pianists who grabbed our attention were Nat "King" Cole, Hank Jones and Oscar Peterson. But this recording spoke to us in a different way. There was something special. It was Bill Evans.

Bill's piano introduction to "On Green Dolphin Street" defied description. He created an exotic mood that set the stage for all the magnificent solos that followed, including his own. Along with the remaining tracks, those tunes became a daily listening ritual for us and our close friends. The music stirred up emotions we'd never felt before. Unlike the caffeinated meter of bebop, the tempos cantered gracefully—yet the solos burned. The players took advantage of the space (Coltrane notwithstanding), but they reveled in rich harmonies. The dynamics seemed more subdued, yet we felt more peaks in these performances than any others. From that moment on, I was a confirmed Bill Evans fan.

After that, Pat brought home *Kind of Blue*, which we listened to all day, sometimes cutting classes to hide in the band room with the stereo. Mr. Matina was a saint, not only for putting up with this illicit behavior, but for letting Pat choose the disks. In time, more Bill Evans records followed. Soon after, I got hooked on a Riverside sampler LP called *The Soul Of Jazz Piano*. It featured Bill playing his composition "Peace Piece." Again, I sat awed by the mesmerizing beauty and simplicity of Bill's playing. How could he get so much out of just two chords? No one else sounded like that. Eventually we got *Everybody Digs Bill Evans* (which included "Peace Piece" from the sampler disk) and were elated to hear Bill swinging away with bassist Sam Jones and drummer "Philly" Joe Jones on the rest of the album. Bill's LP "Waltz for Debby" followed and his rendition of "My Foolish Heart" stopped me in my tracks. His playing was so compelling, always taking you to a special place where you felt personally connected to him.

Meanwhile, I played gigs with many older musicians, all known by my parents. They would pick me up at home with my drums and drop me off safely after the job. I wasn't studying formally with anyone, but my friend Bob LaDelfa showed me a lot and let me sit in on his jobs.

Pat graduated from high school in 1962 and headed off to Potsdam Teachers' College, part of the vast State University of New York system. He lasted for one semester and dropped out. It was the wrong place for a guy who sought to play professionally. My parents were devastated;

they thought he'd made a big mistake. As much as they loved music, they had no way of comprehending what it would take to be a professional or perhaps *maybe they knew all too well*! My father always had a day job to support himself and the family. But Pat had heard about the Berklee College of Music in Boston, a school devoted to jazz. This seemed like the right fit. After taking a semester off, working a job and saving some cash, Pat bought a new horn, applied and was admitted. Berklee turned out to be all that Pat had hoped for and more, so he encouraged both John and me to attend. He ultimately left, one course shy of graduating to play with Buddy Rich's band but went back later and completed his bachelor's degree. John finished high school in 1963 and also started at Potsdam. He lasted about five semesters and then transferred to Berklee.

By the time I was 12, my brothers and I were playing jazz in the basement every day. When John left for college, I was 15, but no one in my peer group played that music. So for me it was playing along with records and gigging with older musicians. I soon found myself gigging with adults. I graduated from high school in 1966 and headed to Berklee. Pat strongly recommended it, and it seemed like the best choice especially after learning that I would study drums with Alan Dawson. I'd heard Alan tear it up on Booker Ervin and Jaki Byard records, so I knew this was the guy I wanted to study with. I was also happy to be with my brothers, who had paved the way for me since I was 5. Moving to a large city like Boston was both exciting and terrifying. But I knew my brothers would look out for me.

Little did I know that I would cross paths with Bill Evans during my brief stay in Boston.

Chapter 2

Berklee (and Bill)
September 1966 to December 1967

ife in a city the size of Boston was shocking for a kid from the sticks of rural, upstate New York. I'd never heard so many sirens and just plain racket at night. Eventually, I learned the ropes, including where to walk and *not* walk alone. I lived in Berklee's dorms—a converted hotel from a bygone era. The rooms were small: three bunk beds and one bathroom. Somehow we made it work. The guys next door were friends. One weekend, they headed home and made the mistake of leaving the window open. On Sunday night, I awoke to one of them yelling and chasing a pigeon down the hall. The winged intruder got in while they were gone and crapped all over the place!

Mishaps in the dorms aside, the fall of 1966 was a great time to study jazz at Berklee. The faculty was top shelf, including such luminaries as trumpeter Herb Pomeroy, trombonist Phil Wilson, pianist Ray Santisi, bassist John Neves and saxophonists John LaPorta, Jimmy Mosher, Charlie Mariano and Andy McGhee. They were the real deal; all boasted lengthy resumes. Pomeroy, LaPorta, Mosher and Wilson also taught arranging and composition. Pomeroy, in particular, was an inspiration to me, even though I was never enrolled in his classes. Occasionally I'd sub in his ensembles, and he always encouraged me. Mosher and LaPorta hired me for gigs outside of school and remained life-long friends.

Best of all were my lessons with Alan Dawson, who turned out to be a most generous, patient, and knowledgeable teacher willing to share anything and everything about jazz and jazz drumming. To this very day, I use the lessons I received from Alan for my own students.

Today, my classmates would read like a who's who of established veterans, including guitarists John Abercrombie and Mick Goodrick; bassists George Mraz, Miroslav Vitouš, Calvin Hill and Rick Laird (although better known for his work on electric bass, he was a fantastic upright player); pianists Richie Beirach and Alan Broadbent; and drummer Harvey Mason. Like everyone else in those days, Harvey was playing straight-ahead jazz; he would develop a healthy interest in funk and pop music later and go on to an incredible career as an L.A. session musician.

Broadbent and Beirach weren't the only great pianists at school though. There were many who would not become as well known but were fine players, nonetheless, such as Mike Hughes, Masahiko Satoh and Carl Schroeder (who would later become Sarah Vaughan's longtime accompanist and musical director). Mike Hughes and I would frequently jam, often imitating concepts pioneered by Bill Evans' groups: the open, non-walking time feel; the conversational approach to group improvisation between all three players; and for the drums, of course, using wire brushes.

I also played a lot with my brothers, John and Pat. On a number of occasions we got calls from the late Fred Taylor, who managed a popular club in town called the Jazz Workshop. Fred always wanted opening acts, so he often called my brothers and me to put a group together whenever he was in a jam; sometimes acts pulled a no show.[1] One time we played opposite Rahsaan Roland Kirk. Another time, we opened for Art Farmer and Jimmy Heath. Yet another time, we covered when Wynton Kelly Trio was scheduled to perform. Wynton suffered from epilepsy and on opening night had a seizure and couldn't go on. Fred called up and said, "Come on down and play." At the Wynton Kelly gig, we met bassist Paul Chambers and legendary drummer Jimmy Cobb, musicians we'd listened to extensively on recordings. I played on Jimmy's drums, which included *the* cymbal he used on Miles Davis' *Kind of Blue* recording. He was very gracious. A few clubs in town offered jazz, but only the Workshop (on Boylston Street) and a club just outside town called Lennie's on the Turnpike (in sleepy Peabody, north of Boston) featured nationally known artists.

And so in the fall of 1967, during the first semester of my sophomore year, Bill Evans was scheduled to play at the Jazz Workshop. Bassist Eddie Gomez and drummer "Philly" Joe Jones (one of my greatest influences) were scheduled to play with Bill, and I wasn't going to miss an opportunity to see and hear two of my idols live. By then, my brothers and I owned several Bill Evans' recordings, including *Everybody Digs Bill Evans* and *Interplay*. Safe to say, we were big fans.

My brothers and I arrived at the club and got our usual seats against the wall, facing the bandstand. Bill and Eddie took the stage at 9:00 p.m., but "Philly" Joe was nowhere in sight. The drums sat there, ready to be played. And Bill had to start because if nothing else, he was going to fulfill his commitment. I think Philly showed up on his own time, and I figured Bill was used to it at this point.

This created one of the earliest dilemmas in my young life. Bill and Eddie played about two tunes, and I sat there in a state of conflict. I thought … well, I could actually get up and get on the bandstand and just start playing. Fred Taylor knew me and would likely vouch for my ability. Also, I had just played a gig that previous summer with Chuck Israels, a former Bill Evans bassist (more on that later). And Chuck told me that he thought Bill would dig my playing.

Here was my dilemma: Do I climb on the bandstand and play Philly's drums or just stay in my seat and listen to Bill and Eddie? By the end of the second tune, I considered walking up to Bill and saying, "If you like, I'll be happy to play the drums until your drummer gets here." But Philly finally arrived, and I stayed seated, figuring that having never met Bill or Eddie, it would not be appropriate to bogart my way on stage. In my heart I realized it would have been the wrong thing to do. It's not a Hollywood picture where you rocket to stardom. (For lay readers, there's an unspoken etiquette to "sitting in": it's a privilege, not an entitlement. One never asks; you are invited.) In the end, I kept my seat out of consideration for the music. I would cross paths with Bill Evans again, and well before my audition for him in 1978.

Meanwhile, the summer gig I just mentioned became a significant catalyst in my life as a professional musician. Instead of returning home to Mt. Morris that summer after my first year at Berklee, I stayed in Boston and headed out to Tanglewood in Lenox (summer home of the Boston Symphony Orchestra in the Berkshire Mountains). I landed a gig at the Avaloch Inn with pianist Ron Fransen, bassist Dick Lupino and saxophonist Frank Nizzari—all students at New England Conservatory of Music. The gig was all the more inspiring because across the street was Music Inn, where Gunther Schuller, Max Roach and Bill Evans taught a summer camp at the Lenox School of Jazz during the 1950s.[2]

At Music Inn, Chuck Israels was the leader of the group playing for the summer with guitarist Gene Bertoncini, pianist Hod O'Brian, drummer Arnie Wise and singer Bill Henderson. Turned out that Arnie eventually got bored with the gig and soon they were looking for a new drummer. Chuck heard me at the Avaloch one night and asked if I'd join the band. I asked if we could work it out so I played both gigs. This actually worked for about two weeks until the owner of one of the clubs complained. So then I had to make a choice. Chuck then tapped Gene Gammage, a New York-based pro to take my place at the Avaloch. My brother Pat also joined the Avaloch band when Frank Nizzari dropped out.

Playing with Chuck, Gene and Hod upped my game considerably because they were real pros. The experience whetted my appetite for a similar life. I'd had a taste of what it was like to play at that level and get paid to do it. When I got back to Berklee, my head was not in the game. After one more semester, I got a call from singer Frankie Randall for a gig in Las Vegas. Frankie was opening for Buddy Rich's band, which would back him up. I decided to bail on Berklee and take the gig.

It was a difficult decision and, truthfully, I intended to return to school after making enough money that month to cover the next semester's tuition. But my grades weren't good; I didn't apply myself as a student. And the dean didn't approve my leave of absence. I wish I'd finished at Berklee, but, in retrospect, the experiences that awaited me with Buddy Rich's band and others were rapidly disappearing. And I'm forever grateful that I had those important opportunities.

Chapter 3

Buddy's Buddy
1968 to 1976

If Boston was a wake-up call for a kid from rural New York, then Las Vegas seemed like complete sensory overload. Singer Frankie Randall's gig was at The Sands Hotel and Casino—one of Sin City's legendary entertainment meccas on the Strip and at various times partly owned by crime bosses[1] (at one time, singer Frank Sinatra also owned shares in the business[2]). Frankie Randall, a really good tenor, sang in much the same swing and ballad style as Old Blue Eyes but was also a graduate of The Juilliard School and an excellent pianist as well.

The trio, which included musical director Ted Howe, lived in a suite at the posh hotel. Ted was one of my instructors at Berklee and also an excellent jazz pianist, arranger and composer. The gig lasted a month, but the $1,000 paycheck fell short of Frankie's promise (a big reason why I didn't return to Berklee). After that month, I traveled with Frankie and Buddy's band to Los Angeles for a one-night gig at a now-defunct club called The Factory in Hollywood. While in L.A., I watched Buddy rehearse for the upcoming live recording *Buddy and Soul*, an album on the Pacific Jazz label. I also rehearsed with the band for a project featuring Buddy and the great Indian tabla master Alla Rakha.

Joe La Barbera on drums backing singer Frankie Randall with the Buddy Rich Band at a month-long gig at The Sands Hotel, Las Vegas, January 1968. *Courtesy of Joe La Barbera.*

Playing with Buddy's band was an amazing experience. My brother Pat played tenor sax and John played in the trumpet section through April (he left after that but continued his relationship with Buddy as a principal arranger). A little-known fact about Buddy (except to die-hard fans) was that he didn't read music. He relied on other drummers to read charts with his band so he could learn them by ear; but one listen and Buddy had it down—memorized! I got tasked with that role during my stint with Frankie Randall. During that time, I got to struggle through such iconic Buddy classics as "Channel One Suite" and "Big Mama Cass." In truth, I mainly kept Buddy's seat warm, but he was grateful and, as previously stated, once the run through was over, he sat down and played it back from memory every time.

Meanwhile, I stood in the wings nightly for every show, soaking up everything he did. It was mind blowing how brilliant this guy was. Occasionally we talked drums and drumming but, needless to say, Buddy was a busy man. If you asked him a serious drum-related question, he was willing to answer and, generally speaking, I always found him easy to be around. But of course, I wasn't working directly for him but rather with him, so there is a big difference. I feel that all the "rant tapes" that have been floating around for years of Buddy yelling at the band are taken out of context. Let's face it, we all have our moments, but because of who he was, these recordings get traction. Keep in mind that no one in his band worked harder every night than he did. Also, Buddy played with every significant jazz artist from Lester Young onward, so his standards were extremely high. Musicians who worked for him may have a different opinion, but that's my take. I was given a glimpse behind the mask of anger he wore on one occasion in Los Angeles at Pacific Jazz studios when the band was rehearsing and recording. A new "band boy" had been hired and was not doing a good job of setting up the drums the way they should have been and Buddy exploded! After a few minutes of this verbal browbeating, I walked over to him and said that I knew how to set them up and would be glad to. He winked and said very quietly, *I know, but if I don't break this guy in right, he will do it wrong every time.*

Meanwhile, back in Las Vegas, the vibe was still fun, and we had our share of lighthearted moments that month. For example, one night during Frankie's set, Buddy came out on stage in a bathrobe and slippers carrying a marching bass drum beating time across the stage and back. He broke everyone up! Another night, as I watched from the front of the house, Buddy arrived at his drums sporting a heavy winter overcoat and without any explanation played the entire set including "West Side Story" wearing it! I rushed backstage after the set and asked him what that was all about, and he told me some guy bet him $5,000 that he couldn't do it. So of course, he had to. Celebrities came nightly, including Jerry Lewis, Alan King and Bill Cosby. That was the way it was back then; if anyone was in town, you went to hear them and say hello.

There were a lot of great musical artists in Vegas that month, including Louis Armstrong and Wayne Cochran and the C.C. Riders. I didn't get to see Armstrong but did go to a late show of the C.C. Riders and they were killing it! Everyone was talking about this young 17-year-old bass player in the band. It turned out to be Jaco Pastorius, and he was hot! I wasn't a big fan of rock back then but hearing this band live made me a believer.

I asked Buddy about my new heroes like Tony Williams and Jack DeJohnette. He said, *I'm sure they're great, but see me in 10 years, and we'll see where they are.* By that I think he was saying it would take more than talent to stay on top of the game. It would take a lot of hard work, commitment and determination. He had respect for any drummer who was dedicated to the art. Of course Tony and Jack have withstood the test of time.

Buddy and I stayed friends for the rest of his life. After I got drafted in the Army, I was asked to sub gigs when he was experiencing severe back pain. This was, of course, contingent on Uncle Sam cooperating with a weekend pass, but it generally worked out. I would meet the band tour bus outside the gates of Fort Dix in New Jersey, where I was stationed. I wound up playing the gig twice. Buddy would always play the first set to satisfy the contract; I'd play the second set. It's hard to imagine the intensity of the pain he was in, but I vividly remember watching him being lifted by two big stage hands onto the drums in the fetal position. Once he was seated, the curtain went up and he played—hard.

There is one gig I did with the band that I will never forget because of the date: July 20, 1969—the day that Neil Armstrong took man's first steps on the moon. I didn't have a weekend pass, so Willard Alexander's office (Buddy's booking agency) contacted the base commander requesting one for me and it worked! I met the bus out front, and we drove into New Jersey for the date. Buddy asked for a television set in his dressing room and timed the sets so that we could all watch it. This was 1969, so it was a black and white TV but everyone was riveted to it—one of those memories that never leaves you. Another memorable event that weekend occurred on the way back to Fort Dix. It was raining as we drove along the New Jersey Turnpike when all of a sudden a car pulled out of a rest stop and right in front of the bus. The bus driver was an ace, but we still bounced off the guardrails on the left and after a lot of skidding landed on the right shoulder, nearly completely tipped over. Miraculously, no one was injured and as we all crawled off the bus, Buddy was standing there shaking his head in disbelief. Meanwhile, lead trumpet player Mike Price was standing with the couple who were driving the car that hit us. They were elderly and quite shaken up, so Mike lightened the mood by quipping, "So, have you run into any other big bands lately?" Musician's humor!

After the gig ended with Frankie Randall, I moved to Rochester, an hour north of Mt. Morris, my home town. At that time, Rochester's music scene was thriving, fueled by an influx of second-generation immigrants with easy access to instruments and lessons. In our area, the Italian community was huge and comprised a substantial portion of the musical roster. Globally, some obvious examples would include violinist Joe Venuti, and guitarists Eddie Lang (born Salvatore Massaro) and Bucky Pizzarelli, and pianist George Wallington (born Giacinto Figlia in Palermo). I was surprised to learn years later on a gig that bassist Peter Washington, too, has Sicilian roots. On the local upstate New York scene, the Mangione Brothers, Chuck and Gap (trumpet and piano, respectively), saxophonist Joe Romano, drummer Roy McCurdy and bassist Ron Carter (who attended the local Eastman School of Music) all were part of the music scene in Rochester back then. Some of the first live jazz performances my brothers and I heard featured Chuck and Gap.

By the time I encountered Chuck's quartet, it featured Gerry Niewood on saxes and flute, Allen Murphy on bass and Vinnie Ruggiero on drums. Gap led a trio with bassist Tony Levin and drummer Steve Gadd (both Eastman students). In 1968, Steve enlisted in the Army, and Gap called to offer the gig, as a replacement. Gap is a very organized band leader with a commercial book for dance gigs and a swinging jazz book—and is still at it. Back then, work was plentiful. From Tuesday through Friday, we'd play afternoons at the Shakespeare Lounge in Xerox Square. Chuck's band would play the evening set. At night (through Saturdays), we'd play at another club.

In November 1968, Bill Byrne, Woody Herman's road manager, called, asking if I was interested in joining the band. Of course I was interested in joining Woody's band but couldn't, because I had been drafted into the Army on November 6, 1968. Fortunately I was assigned to the 173rd Army Band at Fort Dix, New Jersey. This was a typical post band where I played lots of marches, parades and induction ceremonies with some good musicians. I mostly played in the Army concert band and with a small jazz combo. When I wasn't doing that, I was jamming and playing jazz gigs. The proximity to New York City made it possible to head there on weekend passes to catch live bands led by the likes of Miles Davis, Joe Henderson, Freddie Hubbard and McCoy Tyner, which I did quite often. When I think back on all the lives lost during these years and how I was lucky enough to safely stay stateside, it gives me pause. Bill Evans had a similar reflection in 1954.

After my two-year stint in the Army, I returned to Rochester and played Gap's gig for a few months until Woody Herman called again in 1971. I spent a year with Woody's Thundering Herd. This was one of those experiences I wish every jazz drummer could have. He was such a great bandleader—very patient. Woody loved nothing more than to hear a good soloist blow and he would let them! The list of great tenor players that worked for him is a mile long and included saxophonists Stan Getz, Al Cohn, Zoot Sims, Sal Nistico, Frank Tiberi, Gordon Brisker, Gregory Herbert and Joe Lovano. There were other fine soloists throughout the years like Phil Wilson on trombone, John Hicks on piano and Paul Fontaine on trumpet. Prior to 1970, big bands like those led by Woody, Maynard Ferguson and Stan Kenton featured veteran players in all the chairs. But shortly before I joined Woody's band, finances started getting thin, and the jobs became entry-level gigs for college graduates (older, seasoned veterans still held down lead section chairs). But Woody's commitment and enthusiasm never wavered, and as long as you could cut your parts, he was OK. Keeping a big band working on the road was a full-time job and very expensive.

Joe La Barbera playing drums with Woody Herman (clarinet), c. 1972. I don't recall the location, but it was early on in my tenure, based on the personnel which included, front row L-R, Steve Lederer (tenor saxophone), Frank Tiberi (tenor saxophone), Woody Herman (clarinet) and Tom Anastas (baritone saxophone). *Courtesy of Joe La Barbera.*

The cost of the bus alone could break you, so it was important to keep the calendar full. In my first year with Woody, the itinerary was wall-to-wall dates all over the country and they included dances, concerts and jazz venues.

Woody's band played great arrangements for dances and concerts, and the dance book was as much fun as the jazz book! In 1972, I played with Woody at the Newport Jazz Festival. The gig was billed as a reunion with past alumni, including saxophonists Stan Getz and Al Cohn and bassist Chubby Jackson. Backstage, I briefly chatted with a then 19-year-old Peter Erskine, who was making his drumming debut with Stan Kenton's band and admitted to being a little nervous. He did a great job!

Drummer Peter Erskine recalled that day ...

I remember the exact day I met Joe La Barbera—July 3, 1972. This was the day I auditioned for the Stan Kenton Orchestra gig.

As I wrote in my book *No Beethoven*, "The Kenton band does not know that I am auditioning; as far as most of them are concerned, June Christy has brought in a young, long-haired, hippie drummer. Poor June Christy has no idea what is going on with this other drummer sitting down to sight-read her charts and play with the band. Stan counts off the first of her six charts we'll run down, and I give it everything I've got, necessarily so because this drum set I'm sitting-in on has the biggest cymbals I've ever seen or played in my life, and this band is really loud—on top of which I'm trying to make a strong, if not good, impression!"

"I guess I did okay at the rehearsal/audition, because I'm advised of when the concert will begin that evening—my first gig with what will turn out to be June Christy's final appearance with Stan—and, further, I'm told that I should pack my bags and meet the band a week or so later to become the drummer for the Stan Kenton Orchestra."

"Joe La Barbera is drumming for Woody Herman that night, and he is very kind and encouraging to me."[3]

He was also a long-haired hippie-looking drummer at the time. And I must have gravitated towards him recognizing a kindred spirit. But I was also looking for some sense of reassurance or validation, not really sure of what I was doing there all of a sudden in this gathering of road warrior, touring musicians … some of them young and hairy, some of them older and not necessarily wiser and all of them grizzled. Joe must have sensed the bewilderment in my eyes and, as is so much his nature, he came to me to restore a sense of balance, if only for a fleeting moment.

Joe La Barbera is a master of balance. I'm not talking about dynamics so much as that intuitive sense and ability to control the push and pull necessary to bring a piece of music alive. Sure, that's important in a big band, but it's critical in a piano trio. And Joe La Barbera would be one of the first of the big band road musicians (where we were all students, really) to graduate into the Big Leagues and drum for Bill Evans. To extend the baseball analogy, that's like going from a good farm team to batting second or third for the Yankees in the first inning. Not that Joe had that far to travel, as he was already a master of the small-group thing, and he brought that swinging sensibility to the Woody Herman big band.

Hearing him play that night in 1972, I was filled with admiration and awe for what this guy could do, and he inspired me to strive for the same level of excellence. It took me a while. But whenever the miles seemed like too many, the number of gigs, too much … I would always remember the kindness that Joe showed me my first time "up to bat."[4]

Years later I would come to realize just how important having Woody's band on your resume would be. So many players passed through his "Herds" and they all knew that if you worked for Woody, you could play! I made a few lasting friendships on that band, including Harold Danko and tenor saxophonist Gregory Herbert. Harold and I actually met in the Army, and we would eventually share a loft in New York City and do a lot of playing together. Gregory tragically died in a drug mishap, a huge personal and musical loss. Another very important friendship is with Alphonso Johnson who took over the bass chair about midway through my time with Woody. Tall, thin and totally swinging, he began playing upright with the band on the swing tunes and electric on the funk stuff, both killing. I believe he was

Peter Erskine and Joe La Barbera, c. 2017, at University of Southern California, where Peter teaches after a drum clinic. *Courtesy of Peter Erskine.*

only 19 years old when he joined us. Gradually he just stayed on electric, and that was fine with me. We continued our relationship in the next phase of my career with Chuck Mangione. When the bass chair opened up, I recommended Alphonso, and he fit in perfectly. We did get to make one recording with Woody together, *The Raven Speaks*.

Alphonso Johnson recalled those days ...

I remember when Joe and I were traveling and playing with Woody Herman's Big Band. Like most big bands from this period, it was a year full of hit and runs, where we would play the gig, then drive all night on a bus to the next city, and rest for a few hours, do a sound check, play the gig, and repeat the same sequence for another day. One thing Joe would always tell me was, "When the band is tired from all the traveling, they would swing the most." He was so right, the horn section would lay back and let the rhythm section drive the music, and it was killing. Playing with Joe taught me a lot about how to listen and play behind the soloist and how to keep some energy in reserve when it came time to explode.[5]

Chuck Mangione called me while I was in Woody's band to offer the drum chair in the quartet. I had been a big fan of his music since my teens, and small groups appealed more to me, so I eagerly accepted. As before, I replaced Steve Gadd, who was moving to New York City. Besides Chuck on trumpet and keyboards, Gerry Niewood still held down the woodwind chair, but now the band featured Gene Perla on bass, who was later replaced on my recommendation by Alphonso. We made one record with Chuck, *The Land of Make Believe*, a live orchestra concert from the famed Massey Hall in Toronto. When I moved west to California in 1987, Alphonso and I reconnected and became faculty colleagues at the California Institute of the Arts.

Chuck was ahead of his time with the fusion of jazz and orchestra in a contemporary style. The first big concert, *Friends and Love*, was groundbreaking and stands today as one of the best examples of a true fusion of elements in music. It took place at Eastman Theatre before a packed audience. Besides the all-star ensemble on stage, Chuck had secretly placed a choir around the auditorium who rose to their feet and sang at the very climactic finish. The effect was dazzling and, combined with the great music coming off the stage, created an event that I'm certain no one in the audience that night will ever forget. The performance was faithfully captured on

Joe La Barbera on stage at the Eastman Theater, Rochester, NY, with the Chuck Mangione Band. L-R, Gerry Niewood; Soprano Saxophone; Joe La Barbera, drums; Chuck Mangione; Flugelhorn (and Fender Rhodes keyboard) and Alphonso Johnson, Electric Bass. C. 1973. *Courtesy of Joe La Barbera.*

tape by Mick Guzauski and Dick Zicari, another lifelong friend, and was eventually released on Mercury records. This was the beginning of *Phase Two* for Chuck, a musical journey toward fusion.

I spent four years with Chuck, touring all over the world, including dates in New York (Village Vanguard, The Half Note, Newport Jazz Festival), Los Angeles (The Shrine Auditorium, Donte's), London (Ronnie Scott's) and Finland (Pori Jazz Festival). When Chuck wasn't on the road, I'd pick up gigs around Rochester with players like saxophonist Joe Romano, who was a huge influence on me. I had met Joe when I was 18 and had started gigging in Buffalo with him and trumpeter Sam Noto. I learned a great deal from both of them. These musicians played at such a high musical level and exuded so much confidence that it would permeate the bandstand and make you sound better than you actually were. They were not afraid to put it out there for everyone to hear. They both played with such feeling that sparks always flew when they played together.

During my stint with Chuck, I ran into Bill Evans twice. The first time was about 1974–75 in Toronto where Bill was playing at the club Bourbon Street with Eddie Gomez on bass and Marty Morrell on drums. I was sitting in the audience with Chuck, Alphonso and Gerry. When the set ended, Eddie walked right off the stage, came over and told me that Marty was leaving the trio to settle in Toronto and asked if I'd like to audition. I think he knew my playing from hearing me when Chuck's band shared a previous billing with Bill's trio at The Bottom Line in New York City. This likely wasn't a formal invitation, just a request to audition on a gig.

I was really flattered but passed on it. I wanted to stay with Chuck a little longer. I had been with him for about three years and besides enjoying a close personal friendship, I felt like he was starting to get some traction in his career. He'd been signed to A&M Records, and we were contracted for three albums. Bookings were becoming more consistent. Also, I wasn't sure if playing with Bill was what I wanted at that moment in my career.

The next time I ran into Bill was at the Monterey Jazz Festival in 1975. Chuck was booked to appear on the main stage. Bill was playing with an all-star group, billed as *The Piano Playhouse*, which also featured John Lewis, Marian McPartland and Patrice Rushen.[6]

Before we went on stage with Chuck's band, I spotted Bill backstage off in a corner by himself. He looked a bit dejected, not well. By now, I had seen him perform a number of times, but I had never met him. I wasn't going to let another opportunity go by, so I walked up, stuck out my hand and said, "Bill? Hi. Joe La Barbera. Big fan, admirer, a drummer." He said, hello, and that was about it. Instantly, I could tell he needed some personal time over something. There was something that told me, don't press this—just say hello and move on. I left it at that, content that I'd met one of my heroes.

Another memorable gig with Chuck's quartet took place in Atlanta, Georgia, at the Great Southeast Music Hall, a club in a mall that seated about 150, if memory serves. We were there for a week and performing opposite us was Billy Crystal. At the time, Billy was known for his role on TV's *Soap* but was still doing stand-up comedy and he was great! He worked with a piano player so there were a lot of musical gags. But the standout for me was a bit involving exorcising all the TV shows he watched as a kid from the 1950s, complete with characters from each series. You had to be there.

All of us hung out backstage, and we discovered how knowledgeable Billy was about jazz through his family. His uncle Milt Gabler founded Commodore Records and recorded Billie Holiday, Louis Armstrong, Nat "King" Cole, Ella Fitzgerald and Lionel Hampton, among others.[7] He told us about going to the movies with Billie Holiday and how Dexter Gordon was a frequent visitor at his house. Jazz and comedy are a natural together because they both offer the audience a spontaneous experience. Of course many of the bits comedians use have a framework, but there is room for on the spot ad libs. Over the years, comedians were often paired with jazz bands in clubs. Lord Buckley, Lenny Bruce, Dick Shawn, Flip Wilson, Godfrey Cambridge and Professor Irwin Corey all appeared with jazz musicians.

I stayed with Chuck until 1976. When I joined the band, his music was rooted more in the tradition of swinging bebop jazz, on which I grew up. By now, he was heading more toward a pop-oriented sound. I got to be part of his change in direction, recording 1973's *The Land of Make Believe* (recorded live at Massey Hall in Toronto), 1975's *Chase the Clouds Away* and *Bellavia* shortly after. The recordings I did with Chuck were moderately successful, and I'm proud of all of them (*Chase the Clouds Away* eventually went "Gold"—at least 500,000 albums sold). After I left, Chuck scored a major success in 1977 with the chart-topping instrumental "Feels So Good" which got steady airplay on mainstream Top 40 radio. Playing with Chuck was a substantial period of growth for me; I learned so much and was grateful for the opportunity to be in a small group. But had I stayed, I would have felt like I was moving in the wrong direction. By this time, Gerry Niewood and Alphonso Johnson had both left the band. Gerry moved to New York, and Alphonso joined Weather Report.

I needed to get back in touch with straight-ahead jazz, and there was only one place where I felt I could do that: New York City.

Chapter 4

The Audition
June 1976 to January 1979

By 1979, Bill Evans topped any short list of the most influential jazz musicians of his or any other generation. Since arriving in New York in 1955, he'd piqued ear drums as part of Miles Davis' group (where, despite being denied credit, he'd penned the classic "Blue and Green" on the trumpeter's *Kind of Blue* album); recorded dozens of albums as a leader,[1] earning six Grammy Awards;[2] and won unwavering respect from fans and critics.

But perhaps, more important, Bill reinvented the concept of what a jazz piano trio sounded like by creating a new lexicon of harmony and rhythm that influenced peers and generations of musicians to follow. The idea of three different voices interacting seamlessly in a highly creative and rhythmically freer manner while still adhering to an established form was revolutionary.

Meanwhile, I hit the ground running in New York, and fortunately it didn't take too long to get some gigs. Numerous players in town knew me from my stints with Woody Herman and Chuck Mangione. But it was the week with guitarist Jim Hall and bassist Michael Moore at Sweet Basil, a popular haunt on Seventh Avenue South in Greenwich Village, that did me the most good in terms of networking. Bill Goodwin, a former Gary Burton drummer and good friend, called me to sub for him. Everybody came in to hear the trio, and I made a lot of contacts that week.

I was content, freelancing with several leaders at all the clubs in New York City. A short list at the time included guitarists John Scofield and Jack Wilkins; pianists Bernie Leighton and Hal Galper; trumpeter Randy Brecker and his tenor saxophonist brother, Michael; trumpeter Art Farmer; vocalists Chris Conner, Jackie and Roy, and Jackie Paris and trombonist Bob Brookmeyer.

I lived in a loft in Manhattan's Chelsea district at 23rd Street and Seventh Avenue. Pianist Harold Danko and I bought it from Kenny Werner, another great keyboard virtuoso. Later, Harold and I sold it to saxophonist Joe Lovano and trumpeter Glenn Drewes. While they owned it, the loft went up in an infamous fire, apparently started in a restaurant kitchen a flight below. The heat was so intense that one of Joe Lovano's cymbals stored there melted like a Salvador Dali painting. Miraculously, no one was injured.

I loved living in New York! My rent was $600.00 a month split with Harold Danko, and I had indoor garage parking in the next block for $50.00 a month. We jammed constantly at the loft and never went to bed before 3:00 a.m. From our loft, you simply walked outside to the corner and could catch the subway south a few stops to Greenwich Village where it was all happening for me. Or you could take it north to 42nd St. for Manny's Music, Frank Ippolito's Professional Drum Shop, Barry Greenspan's Drummer's World, Joe Cusatis' Modern Drum Shop, Sam Ash or Henry Adler's. Yes, the loft was cold in winter and hot in summer with cockroaches the size of silver dollars, and we always smelled corned beef and cabbage courtesy of the Blarney Stone directly below us. But I was 26 and living my dream!

By late summer of 1977, vibraphonist Gary Burton hired me for his quartet, which also featured Steve Swallow on bass. John Scofield was playing guitar in the band and recommended me to Gary. During this period, John also took a quartet to the Berlin Jazz Festival and recorded his first album for Enja Records in Munich live at the Domicile Club. Richie Beirach played piano and George Mraz was playing bass. The following year I was back at the Berlin Jazz Festival with Mike Brecker's Quartet which included

Hal Galper and Chip Jackson. I was also a member of Hal's quintet along with Mike and Randy Brecker and Miroslav Vitous. We were the band for opening night of Mike and Randy's new club in the Village, Seventh Ave. South. I played in this club many times before it closed.

So, between The Village Vanguard, Sweet Basil, Seventh Avenue South and Hopper's in the village, Strykers uptown, The Office in Nyack, and Gulliver's in New Jersey, I kept fairly busy. I certainly wasn't getting rich, but I was paying my bills and playing jazz. Like I said, I was living my dream. Around this time, Bill Evans was reforming his trio.

Come early 1978, Bill started auditioning bass players at the Village Vanguard. I stopped in one night on a break from my gig nearby and heard Rufus Reid and George Mraz each play a few tunes. Both sounded great. I think every bass player in town showed up that week, and it was obvious how much they enjoyed playing with Bill.

Michael Moore ended up landing the gig, but he left after only a few months, and word went out again that Bill was looking for a bassist. This time Bill took a recommendation from Fred Crane, a pianist colleague from their college days at Southeastern Louisiana University, who suggested he check out Marc Johnson. Marc, then 24, hailed from North Texas State University, one of the country's premier jazz schools. At that time, he played with Woody Herman's band. Bill hired him and the rest, as they say, is history.

By September 1978, Bill decided to part ways with "Philly" Joe. At the time, Bill was recording the album *Affinity*, a collaboration with Toots Thielemans, the late Belgian harmonica and guitar virtuoso. And I was working with Toots at Hopper's, a club on Sixth Avenue near the Village Vanguard.

One night before we started our first set, I noticed Toots greeting Bill Evans and his longtime manager Helen Keane, who had come to hear the group. In fact, they had come to check me out. Guitarist Joe Puma, an old friend of Bill's, recommended me for the trio. Joe Puma and Bill played and recorded together a lot when Bill first hit the scene in 1955. They obviously enjoyed each other's company off the bandstand too, since they spent many happy hours together at local racetracks. Joe was a marvelous guitar player made all the more noteworthy as he played with an impaired left arm from a stroke. Thanks to my friend Warren Odze I started working with Joe and Bernie Leighton at Jimmy Weston's, a storied nightclub in Manhattan's Midtown East neighborhood, whose clientele included Frank Sinatra and Howard Cosell. Joe was seated in a chair in front of me so I got up to extend my hand and say hello. He looked at me, pointed to my ride cymbal and said, "That's a cymbal." Then he pointed to his ear and said, "This is an ear!" By the end of the set we were musical buddies.

In early January, Helen phoned and asked me to come down to the Vanguard and audition. I was back at Hopper's with Toots, but he timed our sets so that I could audition for Bill at the Vanguard and return in time to finish my gig.

When the break arrived, I walked straight across 12th Street to the Vanguard on Seventh Avenue, down the flight of stairs to the club, said hi to Bill, met Marc, adjusted the drums a bit and we were off. With a baby face and long curly blond locks, Marc looked far younger than his 24 years. But he sure played his butt off! Bill exuded so much confidence and was so clear with his direction on every tune that it was quite easy for me to fit in. I was very confident going into the club, having just finished my set with Toots as well as all the other playing I'd done since arriving in New York (Jim Hall, John Scofield, Gary Burton, Michael and Randy Brecker). I can't exactly put into words what I was feeling at the moment, but I'm sure a sense of exhilaration would not have been a bad guess.

Quite honestly, that feeling would return time and again with him once I landed the job. We played the Vanguard at least a half dozen times, and I would still get that feeling. It was always exciting because Bill Evans in my mind was head and shoulders above almost everybody else in the music business. I wasn't nervous at all that night—probably because I'd already established myself in New York and wasn't really *looking* for the gig. Bill didn't say a word about the music we would play but rather just started playing, and I was expected to follow. There were no drum parts, only bass parts for Marc, so I was forced to rely strictly on my ears and eyes. This would turn out to be the only way we would play music together going forward. We never had any rehearsals unless it was with someone outside the trio. I don't remember all the tunes we played except that we closed with

"My Romance," and I got through Bill's famous arrangement, which involved trading solos with Marc and Bill. But what I won't forget is that playing with Bill and Marc immediately felt great. After the set Bill walked by me and said, "Hey man, have you been checking out my book? You seemed to know everything we played." The truth, of course, is that I'd been a fan most of my life, and while I may not have known exact arrangements, I think I knew what to do in terms of accompanying the man.

Bassist Marc Johnson recalled the audition ...

I remember there was a guitar player, Joe Puma, who recommended Joe, and just based on that recommendation, Bill was predisposed to having him in the group. But after he sat in, that was the clincher. I was trying to get Steve Houghton on the gig. I didn't know Joe. Steve sounded like Marty Morell, but Joe was more seasoned and had wider experience. I don't remember the audition. But Joe impressed Bill, I know that. It wasn't my decision to make, and I was just grateful to be there. Bill didn't ask my opinion. I don't know if Helen was in the room. Maybe she chimed in.[3]

A few days later, Helen called again and asked me to play a week with the trio at the Bijou Café in Philadelphia (a one-time hotel whose former residents included singer Billie Holiday[4]). Turned out that Bill was booked at the Bijou opposite Art Blakey and the Jazz Messengers, and I was thrilled to share the stage with both men. So in January 1979, I started with that gig. Bill drove himself down there while I picked up Marc and Helen in my trusty, red 1971 Volvo 142-S.

On the way down, Helen asked if I would stay with the trio on a permanent basis. At this point in my life, I had been on the road with Woody Herman for a year, Chuck Mangione for four years and close to a year with Gary Burton. I was beginning to get some minor studio work in New York. Most drummers in town were looking at all the studio work and saying, "That's the future." Arranger-composer Don Sebesky hired me for some jingles. I also played on a remake of the original Maxwell House coffee ad. For that, it

Marc Johnson in Rome, Italy, c. 1980, packing up his bass after a show in Europe. Marc was 24, a graduate of the North Texas State University music program, and a veteran of Woody Herman's Thundering Herd, when Bill hired him for the bass chair. *Courtesy of Joe La Barbera.*

was just me with a wood block and a microphone. I started improvising, and the first thing I heard from the booth is, "Don't be so creative. Just read the notes. It's a percolator, buddy. It's not Elvin Jones." By then, I was still rotating in and out of several clubs, including the Village Vanguard, Sweet Basil, Seventh Avenue South, Hopper's and Stryker's. I really wanted to put down some roots in New York, and as any studio musician will tell you, if you travel, the contractors forget about you quickly.

I was also newly married and had moved out of my 23rd Street digs to a smaller loft on Center Street and Grand Avenue, right where Little Italy and Chinatown meet in a head-on collision. My gig with Gary Burton ended abruptly when he disbanded the group right before Christmas. While getting sacked from a great band stung, particularly during the holidays, Gary said it wasn't personal. He often got to a point where he needed a fresh start with personnel. Fortunately right after that, tenor saxophonist Joe Farrell hired John Scofield, who once again got me on that gig.

So with marriage, I was *seriously* seeking stability. You can work as a sideman for the rest of your days, but in that life, you'll get gigs, you'll lose gigs and you'll travel for long periods of time—away from home. I knew what the road was like. It doesn't change ... ever. The only reward is the music, and that doesn't always put food on the table. I wanted to get my foot in the door in New York like all my other friends and join the cadre of working musicians that were doing recording sessions—so I could stay in town and provide for my family. That's what I had initially told Helen, and she understood and thanked me for being up front about it.

After that week at the Bijou, my feelings changed because of what we experienced on the bandstand. The trio with Bill and Marc gelled quickly, and people in the audience sensed it. So did we. There is a novelty of sorts about "all-star" groups where each member is a well-known giant, but somehow it doesn't always yield the best results. Without mentioning names, I think we've all heard groups that looked great on paper but simply lacked the chemistry to play good music. Certainly, Marc and I were not stars or even well known yet, but the alchemy with Bill was great right from the start. I know Bill felt it simply by the way the music grew night to night in subtle ways.

Communicating on the bandstand was effortless, mainly because Bill made it so easy to just be yourself and play. We all found ourselves anticipating and reacting to one another's musical ideas at the right moment, and the time-feel settled in nicely. I didn't expect the broad dynamic range that Bill allowed me, and I sensed immediately that everything I played influenced the music. I could watch and hear Bill juggling input from Marc and me with ease, weaving it seamlessly into his own ideas and making us sound as one. Playing drums in a trio differs slightly from other-sized ensembles, but the fundamentals are always the same: serve the music. I once told Buddy Rich that I wanted to be a "small group drummer," and he scoffed at the notion, saying "if you're a drummer you do it all, big groups and small." He was so right. I didn't really have to make a lot of adjustments to my playing when I joined Bill. Very quickly I discovered that he allowed for any reasonable musical interaction. He gave you so much room to grow, provided you were respectful of the music.

This kind of communication really defines jazz, and it only comes from a commitment to the music. If it was feeling this good this early on, then it could only get better with time. By the end of the engagement and

Pianist John di Martino was 20 years old when he caught a late set with Bill's new trio at the Bijou that week. The Philadelphia native invited a former girlfriend to join him at the club, where they had a few drinks and fell in love with Evans and his new trio. "I was in a state of rapture listening to the music," said di Martino, who has worked with saxophonist Houston Person, singer Freddie Cole and percussionist Ray Barretto. "I remember peeking at Marc's music stand, and there were a lot of scribbled changes. It looked like something Bill wrote on an airplane."

After the set, he approached Bill to ask a few questions. "I just had an affectionate way of grabbing people by the arms," di Martino said of trying to query the pianist. "Bill groaned and kept walking." Joe and Marc laughed, seeming to take it in stride. "I remember asking them if they ever rehearse, and they just chuckled."[5]

New York pianist John Di Martino was in high school when he went to hear the Bill Evans Trio at the Bijou Café in Philadelphia. It was Joe's first gig with Bill. *Photo by Janis Wilkins. Courtesy of John Di Martino.*

after talking it over with my wife, I decided to stay with the trio. On one of the breaks toward the end of our stay, Bill asked if I'd made a decision. I told him that I wanted to be part of the music, which seemed to please him as well. In reaching this decision, I embraced my roots in jazz. Playing it is what got me into music in the first place. And while I longed for the fiscal stability a life in the studios might bring, in my heart I knew I wasn't cut out for session work as a career. Quite frankly, I wasn't that great at reading and wasn't up on the latest trends in pop music. Playing jazz was what drew me into a life as a musician, and in the end, it has always steered me on the right path. And what Bill offered was exactly what I wanted—playing music of that quality—if you're lucky enough to get the chance. I couldn't pass it up.

Chapter 5

On the Road Again
January–April 1979

After the gig in Philadelphia, we returned home to New York, and I soon got a phone call from Helen Keane to confirm: *Would I join the trio?* I told her that the two weeks in Philadelphia really helped me to make a decision, and that I would accept the offer. It was just so great to play with Bill and Marc and feel that energy from the audience. I'd felt it before with Chuck Mangione—when the crowd shows you they're into it. It's a powerful high. It taps into an urge, the reason why you play music in the first place. You love the music. You love that feeling of making something happen. All during the gig at the Bijou, I felt something so positive. Bill Evans was one of my heroes. Playing something that he was digging and the audience was digging was a thrill. I told Helen I would definitely stay.

Later that month we took off for Chicago, and on January 23, we made the first of three visits to Rick's Cafe Americain. Situated in the lobby of a Holiday Inn on Lake Shore Drive, Rick's was run by Jerry Kaye, a big, burly Chicago cop by day and jazz impresario by night. If the club's name suggests the classic Humphrey Bogart film, *Casablanca*, it was intentional. Jerry dressed in a white dinner jacket and bow tie like Bogie's Rick. He also booked and introduced the bands and laid down

Bill Evans Trio on stage at Rick's Café Americain, Chicago, Illinois, January 1979. Both Marc Johnson and Gary Novak recount fond memories of this performance. *Photo by Steve Kagan. Courtesy of Steve Kagan.*

Bill Evans Trio on a break from the gig at Rick's Café Americain. Although we are not wearing jackets, our host Jerry Kaye always appeared in a white dinner jacket and bow tie, a la Humphrey Bogart in *Casablanca*. *Photo by Steve Kagan. Courtesy of Steve Kagan.*

club rules—meaning he didn't suffer fools who talked over the music. He'd issue one warning and if they didn't comply, he personally showed them the door. He ran that place the way it was supposed to be run. We became good friends, and even after Bill died, whenever I was in Chicago, I'd look him up. January 1979 was a very severe winter even by Chicago standards, and we experienced a storm that literally closed the city down. Snow drifts blanketed all the streets, leaving cars unable to move. In my hotel room, I woke to deafening silence on Lakeshore Drive, normally among Chicago's busiest thoroughfares.

We would play Rick's twice more, including a stop in April 1980 with more accommodating weather. During that visit, John Belushi and Dan Aykroyd were around the corner at a city pier, shooting scenes for *The Blues Brothers* movie. At night, several band members, including saxophonist "Blue" Lou Marini, came in to hear us. I also recall the second visit because an airshow was in town. During the day, fighter jets buzzed my hotel room window, including an AV-8B Harrier like the one featured in the Arnold Schwarzenegger movie, *True Lies*. Imagine looking out your 10th-floor window onto Lake Michigan, and suddenly a fighter jet is staring directly at you!

Meanwhile, the trio's energy continued to grow. Word was out on Bill's latest group, and people came to hear the band during our two-week run. The place was doing really good business. Better still, we were connecting with people and feeling good about the trio's development.

Marc Johnson recalled that gig …

We were performing in Chicago at Rick's Cafe Americain, which was located inside the Holiday Inn on North Lake Shore Drive. I remember the venue as *DownBeat* magazine sent a photographer there during the engagement to photograph the trio in conjunction with an article and interview with Bill.

We had finished one of our sets, and I went to the bar to have a Coca-Cola. I was sipping my drink when a fellow in a business suit approached me. He told me he was a farmer, staying in the hotel and was in town to meet with a banker about business. Being that Rick's Cafe was the nearest source of live entertainment, he sauntered in. He said, "You know, I never heard live jazz before. I've got to tell you, that was like some kind of religious experience."

Without intending to sound melodramatic, taking the stage with Bill and Joe was like going to church. The bandstand was our sanctuary, a solemn place that offered the opportunity for spiritual transcendence. I really felt this way then, and that relationship to creating music on stage continues to this day wherever and with whomever I am performing. There is something wonderfully fulfilling to be in that focused "now" moment of creating while feeling in your heart that what you are striving for is what you most want to be doing. In the most perfectly immersed moments, the sensation feels as though some higher power is at work. Perhaps, on occasions, some sense of this is conveyed to the audience, especially in light of what that farmer told me so many years ago.[1]

I didn't witness this exchange, Marc told me about it later. But I was flabbergasted to hear a comment like that. It not only demonstrated the powerful ability of jazz to communicate, but it spoke volumes about Bill and the trio; we were working together so well, the music was reaching people. That happened night after night. Also, Marc's comment—that he now feels that transcendence today no matter who he's performing with—is exactly the lesson I learned as well working with Bill and Marc.

During this engagement at Rick's, one of Bill's Army buddies, Larry Novak showed up. Larry, Bill and another Chicago pianist named Sam Distefano were all in the 5th Army Band and remained very close. Larry brought his 11-year-old son to the gig.

Gary Novak recalled the first time he heard Bill Evans in concert ...

My first exposure to Bill Evans was through my parents, pianists Larry and Carol Novak. The story starts with my father's dear friend and my godfather, Sam Distefano. Also from Chicago, Sam became the entertainment director for Playboy, then went to do the same at the Riviera Hotel and Casino in Las Vegas.

Sam and Bill were bunk mates in the Army for basic training at Fort Sheridan during the Korean War. I think this was in 1952. By joining the 5th Army Band to avoid the draft, Bill basically saved Sam's life. In roughly 48 hours, Bill taught Sam to play the flute well enough to march in the Army band, which ultimately led to Sam introducing my parents to one another shortly after. Sam introduced Bill to my father around that time and they quickly became friends.

Not long after Bill enlisted, my father's draft number came up, and Fort Sheridan was in his future, too. Following the advice of Bill and Sam, my father immediately learned to play trombone and also joined the 5th Army Band, avoiding active duty. The caring nature of Bill wanting to keep his friend from active duty is quite possibly the reason I exist.

Growing up in a Chicago household of two jazz pianists, Bill's music was sacred in our house. When I started playing drums, the music

I was exposed to was all Bill. My first emotional reaction to a live performance was at 11 years old. My parents took me downtown to see Bill at a club in Chicago on Lake Shore Drive called Rick's Café Americain. My father had done several trio performances there, as had my mother, so it was a familiar spot for me as a kid. The owner Jerry was very nice to my dad and always took care of me as a kid. If I remember correctly, Jerry was a Chicago police officer. Dad never had to worry about parking tickets when he played at Rick's.

Around April 1980, I remember my parents taking me to see Bill's trio with Joe and Marc Johnson. I remember the music like it was yesterday. I was only 11, but I knew I was witnessing something very special. I remember the audience being mesmerized by the mastery and emotion. That particular lineup changed my father's musical life and subsequently mine as well. I am forever grateful to have witnessed something so special. I walked away with the idea of time being felt and not dictated. The openness of the music was profound—even to an 11 year old.

My parent's relationship with Bill was something I didn't truly understand until I was a little older. He visited the house with Sam quite a few times, and I was lucky enough to play "My Romance" and "How My Heart Sings" with Bill in our basement. Bill would play my dad's Rhodes, which was set up in my practice room. Many musicians would come to the house to socialize, cook, rehearse or enjoy some general fun. When Bill was in town, my parents would always make sure to see their friend. I was a very lucky jazz kid.[2]

A few years later, I would be invited to the Novak home and have the opportunity to hear young Gary play, and he was swinging already on drums and piano. Today we are friends and neighbors in Los Angeles. Anyone who follows the music scene will know that Gary Novak today is one of the outstanding drummers on the scene.

On January 30, we headed to Ames, Iowa, and recorded a live concert. It was part of a series called *Jazz at the Maintenance Shop*, filmed at Iowa

Los Angeles drummer Gary Novak first heard Bill Evans in Chicago when he was 11 years old. Novak's parents were friends of Bill's, who often stopped by their house. As a child, Gary jammed with Bill several times in his basement. *Photo by Alex Solca. Courtesy of Gary Novak.*

State University and broadcast later on public television (our performance can be found on YouTube). Numerous jazz legends played this concert series, including saxophonists Phil Woods and Dexter Gordon. I remember the night well because it was brutally cold outside. Inside the college's Student Union was the "M-Shop," or Maintenance Shop, a 195-seat club.[3]

Upon arriving, however, we got an unwelcome surprise. In those days, Bill asked for a Baldwin piano at least 7 feet long for a club and 9 feet for a concert hall. I can't recall what was in its place, but it was an inferior piano, especially for a performance that was being videotaped for broadcast. Bill liked Steinways but played Baldwins because the company provided them to artists on the road. Steinway would not do that for all their artists (maybe for classical virtuosos like Arthur Rubinstein but not necessarily for jazz artists like Bill). So the piano he got was a drag. And he was upset. It's one thing to deliver a different manufacturer's piano, but if it's not in good shape, that's not helpful. And I remember that that piano didn't have much of a low end, and Bill worked down in that register quite a bit.

Nonetheless, we did a lengthy sound check, getting the sound just right and allowing the camera crew to plot angles for the band. But when we returned for the show, the staff had moved the tables, blocking all the camera angles. Worse still, the sound was now poor. Bill was getting feedback in his monitor. During the show, Bill let slip a few comments about the sound and piano. "This tune is supposed to be a tender waltz," he said, right before "Gary's Waltz," but "there may be some hostile frustration in it because I'm dealing with a piano that I'm not too happy with. But we'll do the best we can." Before playing "Suicide is Painless (Theme From MASH)," Bill asked for more bass in the monitors but apparently got too much. After the tune, Bill looked straight at the soundman and said, "It's too boomy." Then, with undisguised sarcasm and shaking his head, he added, "I'm glad we had a sound check. We spent about a half hour down here getting it right." The crowd responded with some good-natured laughs. "But we'll just go ahead and weather it through because that's our job."

I know some people got the impression from this that Bill was difficult to work with. In fact, he was the easiest person of his stature to deal with. Bill would put up with terrible circumstances if they couldn't be prevented. But this didn't have to be. A lot of preparation went into it, and yet somebody dropped the ball along the way. And now the artist had to deal with an inferior piano. Imagine how much better those concerts would have been if he'd had a decent piano? (The individual sets, produced in two segments, first aired locally in Iowa in March and May 1979, according to Iowa Public Television.[4]) Both sets from this concert were eventually released as videos with Set 1 titled *Bill Evans Trio Jazz at the Maintenance Shop* and Set 2 titled *Last Performance*.

Bill Evans Trio during sound check for a show at The Maintenance Shop,
Iowa State University, Ames, Iowa. January 30, 1979. L-R, Bill Evans,
piano; Marc Johnson, bass; Joe La Barbera, drums. *Photo by Liz Havens.*
Photo courtesy of Joe La Barbera.

Sometime later, Bill told me that if the band played well on a given
show, it could lift him out of the doldrums from bad pianos and acoustic
nightmares. You can't predict when that will happen. You can't explain it.
It just demonstrates the power of the music when it's right. Even though
this trio was in its infancy, that's what happened in Ames that night.
I could tell Bill enjoyed the gig because we were all creating a dialogue.
He would pick up rhythmic motifs that I was playing, and I would pick up
rhythmic ideas from him, and we'd hand them off. And you'd know for
sure he loved what Marc played. Sometimes Bill wouldn't comp during
Marc's solos but rather he would close his eyes and a smile would slowly
crease his face. You could tell he was pleased even though the circumstances weren't right (and I'm sure he gave Helen Keane an earful after
that show about the problems we encountered). Considering it was early

Bill Evans during sound check at The Maintenance Shop, Ames, Iowa. January 30, 1979. The piano that was provided was not the instrument agreed upon in the contract, and his displeasure over it was palpable. *Photo by Liz Havens. Courtesy of Joe La Barbera.*

in the band's tenure, I think he ended up feeling like this band was going somewhere.

In the first set, the camera mostly showed Bill and Marc along with several group shots from a distance. At times, you can see tight shots of my hands sweeping brushes while the camera gazes at Bill from afar. By the second tune of the second set, "34 Skidoo," a cameraman made his way around my drum kit and found a spot to film my hands from the side and behind me. More adjustments came later, bringing improved views of the trio from a different angle. These kinds of issues are unnecessary but happen more often than the general public realizes and they added to the mounting frustration the trio felt when we hit the stage. Miraculously it all faded away as the music literally took over.

Ames still stands out for me because I hadn't played on television much (a big reason I was excited about the gig). It finally aired in New York but unfortunately after Bill died. The local Albany, New York PBS station played it at about 3:00 a.m., long before we had VCRs (remember those?), so I stayed up late to watch it, groggy and bleary eyed. Knowing Bill wasn't around to see it left me feeling pretty sad as did a reissue of the recording '58 Miles around the same time.[5] The reason it choked me up was that Bill had played a cassette of this track for me in advance and he was so pleased to hear himself swinging with these giants once again. He told me that the reason Miles called "Love for Sale" was that all the other material that day was quite subdued and Miles could sense that drummer Jimmie Cobb was chafing at the bit to cut loose.

Come spring that year, Bill had a tour lined up in the Pacific Northwest. Our flight plans had us changing planes in San Francisco. But airline machinists had gone on strike.[6] We had a quick discussion about whether or not to proceed. We all agreed to go even though it looked doubtful we'd get beyond San Francisco due to the strike. I think we all just really wanted to play. Once we arrived in San Francisco, Bill booked us into a nice hotel, and I got on the phone with Northwest Airlines and booked our flights into Canada. On April 13, we played the Mayflower Restaurant in Edmonton, which was memorable for two reasons. First of all, it was a desanctified church with a Korean-era fighter jet hanging from the ceiling (who could forget that?!) And, this is the night we met Laurie Verchomin, a waitress for the concert promoter, Railtown Jazz Society. After the show, Bill gave Laurie his phone number on the back of Helen Keane's business card, and when Bill returned to New York, they corresponded and developed a relationship.

Laurie Verchomin recalled that night …

The room was an old church that had been refashioned into a disco cum Chinese restaurant. It was a packed house both nights. The atmosphere was church like—not a lot of glasses clinking. I was wearing a very tight, full-length, black cocktail dress. Joe was seated at the table when Bill and I met. I was serving him. Bill heard my voice first, and that is what attracted him to me (he said later). I asked him if he needed anything, referring to his post-show dinner. He responded that he did … and approached me later on to invite me back to his hotel room. I was excited by his invitation and responded with, "I'd love to. Can I bring my boyfriend? He's a really big fan of yours." To which he answered with a chuckle, "That's not exactly what I had in mind." We went back to my bare room with three chairs and a host of his fans. Bill asked for a Pepsi, which I didn't have. I served him tea in a vintage china cup. Later Bill gave me his phone number written on the back of Helen Keane's business card.[7]

From Edmonton, we drove south to Calgary. The gig was at the Calgary Inn, where we also had rooms for the night. I dropped off my drums while Bill inspected the piano in the hotel ballroom where the April 15 concert was scheduled. The piano at Ames was a letdown, but it was at least playable. The piano at the Calgary Inn was a disaster. Some of the ivories were broken as were some strings inside the harp, where someone had dumped a cigarette ashtray.

Bill saw a man nearby sweeping the floor and asked who was in charge. Turned out he was a board member of Jazz Calgary, the nonprofit organization promoting the event. Bill told him the piano was unsatisfactory. I distinctly remember Bill telling him that if he got a piano tuner to work on the piano until the time the concert was supposed to start that the trio would perform one set. The man reacted defensively and pointed out that he had a contract requiring Bill to perform two sets. Bill countered that he would play one show if the piano was fixed and playable in time for downbeat. With increas-

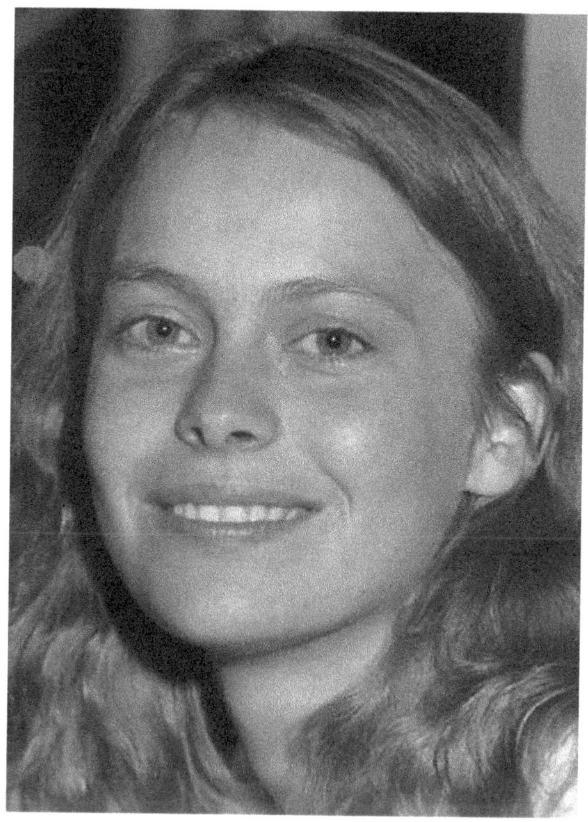

Laurie Verchomin was waitressing at the Mayflower Restaurant in Edmonton, Canada, when she met Bill during a show there in 1979. She eventually moved to New York to live with him until his passing away in 1980. *Photo by Francine Tomlin in 1980. Courtesy of Laurie Verchomin.*

ing hostility, the man said he'd sue Bill if he didn't play. Bill reiterated his position: Repair the piano and make it sound decent by 8:00 p.m., and I'll give you one show. This was at 5:00 p.m.

Unfortunately, for the local fans, nothing was done to improve the piano, not even to try to clean it up. The guy in charge drew his own line in the sand. So at gig time, we came downstairs from our rooms to a lobby packed with fans waiting for the concert. We were dressed for the gig. Bill walked into the ballroom, looked at the piano, came out and shook his head in disapproval in front of us and the crowd of eager patrons.

The three of us walked out the hotel door and across the street where we found a movie theater and caught a flick (Marc Johnson recalled that it might have been Ridley Scott's sci-fi horror thriller *Alien*, which drew no reaction from Bill. In the two years with Bill, we saw three movies together; the aforementioned Sci-Fi classic, Woody Allen's *Manhattan* and *Tom Horn*, a little-known western with Steve McQueen). The local paper lambasted Bill the next day with a headline declaring that Bill Evans didn't care about his fans. The critic, however, didn't bother to look at the actual facts: The promoters supplied an inferior and unacceptable instrument.

Malcolm Page, a longtime Calgary resident and drummer, played numerous gigs at the Calgary Inn and recalled that night …

I showed up in time for the concert, only to find the whole thing had been canceled. A rumor was going around that Bill was ill. Turned out it was the piano. Having played the Inn many times, I knew that piano. It was an old Heintzman & Co. It was just an awful, awful piano. In those days, there weren't many electric keyboards around. This one was disgusting. It would have three beers and a pizza inside it. The piano was in the open all the time, and any Tom, Dick or Harry could bash along on it. I doubt the damned thing was ever tuned.[8]

After hearing the promoter's story (see below), it sounds like there was a breakdown in communication somewhere along the way and I certainly applaud his efforts to get a decent instrument for Bill to play. Bill Evans was a pro. We saw him suffer through an inferior piano in Ames as well as a lengthy sound check which proved futile in the end. I saw the piano in Calgary with my own eyes and distinctly remember thinking that even I wouldn't have played it. In hindsight, perhaps Bill should have told the audience why he canceled the show—because the piano was an unplayable wreck. Perhaps he might have invited them to inspect it for themselves and draw their own conclusions. But he didn't. I think that at that point, he just

Malcolm Page, seen here with Joe, is a Canadian drummer who showed up at the Calgary Inn, April 15, 1979, to hear the Bill Evans trio—only to learn that Bill refused to go on because the piano was unplayable. *Photo by Patti Page. Courtesy of Malcolm Page.*

Tunde Agbi, a Calgary energy company executive, was the president of the board of Jazz Calgary at the time. He recalled that Bill (via manager Helen Keane) requested a Baldwin piano …

"I had a relationship with a piano store that carried Baldwins," Agbi said, "and arranged for one to be brought to the venue." But with less than a week to go, the store reneged, offering "any number of what I would characterize as lame excuses," he said. "I did everything I could to persuade them to do it."

Among the objections voiced by the store: They wouldn't sign off on Jazz Calgary's piano tuner, one of the group's members. Also, store officials apparently didn't know Bill was a Baldwin artist and couldn't reach Helen Keane, Bill's manager, for confirmation, Agbi added.

"From Tuesday prior to the concert, the story was a moving target as to why we may or may not get it. By Thursday, it was clear they wouldn't give us the piano. I tried to call them, and no one took my call. We had to try and make do with what was there. The focus was either the Baldwin or what they had there."

The man that Bill spoke with in the ballroom, Agbi said, was the late Jerry Dziuba, an at-large board member, who volunteered to check out the piano at the hotel and see if it was appropriate. Dziuba did look over the piano and reported back that it was acceptable, Agbi recalled.

"When I showed up to see the concert, Bill said they weren't going to play," Agbi said. "I tried to talk to Bill on the phone. He said he wouldn't play the piano. The equipment was not up to the standard that Bill was comfortable playing. I looked at it, and I thought it would do. It might not have met the high standards that Bill required, but not being the same caliber of musician that Bill was, I thought the concert could go on. So we had to refund money to the guests. It was an unpleasant experience, especially for me as a great fan of Bill's. So I was disappointed."9

figured, *you know what, it's not my job to do that. My job is to play the piano when they give me a good instrument.* So I admire him for sticking to his guns. I backed him up completely. I believe Mr. Agbi was sincere that he thought the piano would do. But the truth is that the piano was trashed. Simply put, there was no excuse for any serious promoter to expect an artist of Bill Evans' stature to play on the piano that was provided—it was utterly ridiculous!

Fortunately before the tour ended, we stopped in Vancouver to perform at the Ridge Theater to a packed house and where Bill played a beautiful baby grand, cared for by a tuner who was absolutely first class in a nice auditorium. The piano sounded great, Bill was inspired and the audience got what they came for, an evening of great music. This concert was recorded for the Canadian Broadcasting Company and aired sometime later that year. Unfortunately, it has never surfaced as a recording.

Two days later, the trio sat down for what was to be a weeklong engagement at Blues Alley, a legendary jazz club in Washington, D.C.'s Georgetown neighborhood. The band opened the run on April 17. Around the first day or so, however, Bill got word that his brother Harry had committed suicide. Bill was very close to Harry (who suffered from schizophrenia) and really admired him.

Marc Johnson recalled the immediate and profound effect this news had on Bill that night ...

I always played with my eyes closed. We were about eight bars into "Re: Person I Knew" when I realized there was no piano coming out. I opened my eyes and found Bill backing up from the piano with tears streaming down his face and saying, "He was too much a part of the music." I didn't know Harry had committed suicide. Bill was maybe a little more private with me than possibly with Joe ... maybe because I was younger. We were supposed to go to the Southwest for clinics, a masterclass and concert after Blues Alley, but that got postponed. That was a horrible time. That was the beginning of the end for Bill.[10]

I also remember that evening at Blues Alley. We'd just started "Re: Person I Knew" when I looked over at Bill who had stopped playing and was in tears. He said something like, *I can't do it* or *can't go on* and left the stage. In the dressing room, he told both Marc and me that Harry had committed suicide. I'm pretty sure that was it for that evening. In an attempt to salvage the gig, the club intended to finish the week-long engagement with Marc Copland (then known as Marc Cohen) subbing the remaining dates for Bill. We wound up playing at least one night with Marc on piano, who remembered that gig well in an email.

Pianist Marc Copland (then known as Marc Cohn) recalls that episode ...

Joe, Marc Johnson and I were scheduled to do the last two or three nights of the week at Blues Alley. Bill's brother Harry died midweek, and it became apparent that Bill was in too much grief to do the gig. The club arranged for the three of us to rehearse. Later that day or the following day, Bill pulled Joe and Marc out because of a dispute over pay with the owner, and I ended up filling in with local cats.

I remember that rehearsal, and here's why: At the time, I was into re-harmonizing the chord schemes of standards, and using those re-harmonizations as a basis for improvisation. I remember speaking with Marc after the rehearsal about some of my charts, which were riddled with reharmonization schemes, and he explained to me that Bill was doing his harmonic stuff over the basic changes. I expressed surprise, and Marc said something like, "You should see Bill's charts, it's all ii-V's, looks very ordinary." Of course Bill didn't *sound* very ordinary. But I had expected his charts—and way of operating—would be like mine.

This got me curious, and over time it became clear that Bill's modus operandi made sense, and was picked up and developed by Herbie Hancock in the early sixties.

It now seemed clear to me that it was more musical to stick with the original chord scheme, more or less, as a framework, and then build voicings and substitutions over those original changes, which is more or less what I've done the last three and a half decades. That rehearsal with Joe and Marc contributed to the development of this aesthetic choice.[11]

Pianist Marc Copland filled in for Bill Evans at Blues Alley in Washington, D.C. after Bill learned of his brother Harry's death. *Photo by Francesco Prandoni. Courtesy of Marc Copland.*

Despite this obvious emotional setback for Bill, the trio continued to blossom. And just like for Marc Copland, Bill turned out to be one of the most important mentors in my musical career.

Chapter 6

Lessons from Bill:
The Joy of Discovery
April–May 1979

big advantage to being around a great musician like Bill Evans was the exposure to all the knowledge he would share, either verbally or simply by playing. He revealed his approach to jazz improvisation in a 1966 video, made with his brother Harry, called *The Creative Process*. In fact, it was something that could be applied to just about any given task. In short, it requires the individual to focus all their attention on a particular thing. To go there, Bill would just mentally "flip a switch on" to begin the process.

It takes some practice, but eventually you can train yourself to be totally "in the moment" when performing, and it allows you to overcome mental and physical fatigue. I can honestly say that I saw this happen on numerous occasions, especially toward the end of Bill's life when his stamina was all but depleted—but he still managed to rise to the occasion.

In a Canadian Broadcasting Company radio interview with Ross Porter in 1980, Bill talked about having a pure inner spirit even though his physical exterior was rapidly deteriorating.[1] Maybe this was the source of his energy. Just to elaborate a bit, Bill felt that during this period in America (1979–80), there was a huge emphasis on physical health and appearances almost to the point of obsession. Bill had nothing against this but felt that, for many, it was a priority over a more wholesome inner self. He fully acknowledged that he was not in good physical health but did possess a pure inner spirit. I would not dispute this view at all. However, in hindsight, it simply pits one obsession against another. When my wife and I were expecting our first child, I felt the need to be more active, so I began running daily. Bill would tease me by announcing that he, too, had done his exercises the night before with several brisk walks to the bathroom! Ironic, really, when you consider what a jock he was in his youth. Football, golf and swimming were all part of his leisure activities, and he looked like your classic *Three Letter Collegian.*

Another concept I found interesting was something Bill called "The Joy of Discovery." I first heard him use this term at a clinic in Tucson, Arizona in the spring of 1979. The trio performed a series of workshops and a concert. I loved this phrase and all it implied from the start. At one point, a student pointedly asked Bill what notes he used in a particular chord voicing on a recording. It's a logical question, and many of us have fielded similar questions about something we may have played on a record.

But Bill's answer was not what any of us expected. He told the student, and I'm paraphrasing here, *I can tell you exactly what I played, but it will have no real meaning for you and you'll probably forget it quickly. What you really need to do is to sit down with the song I played and work through it yourself as I did. Then find things that are personal to you based on your understanding of music to date. If I just tell you what you ask, I will be robbing you of the joy of discovery.* This was a fantastic lesson for me and the kids.

What about the joy of discovery on a professional level? I have definitely made my own discoveries in the practice room and still do today. But Bill offered me and everyone who ever worked with him the opportunity to make discoveries on the bandstand. He did this by never having an agenda beyond full participation by all of us in the group. He did not want you to sound like the person you just replaced (and believe me, some bandleaders do!) but to find your voice within the music for yourself. This requires a leader with

Bill Evans Trio concert poster for a show at the Temple of Music & Art in Tucson, Ariz. This concert was postponed a few days, following the news of the death of Bill's brother, Harry Evans. On the back of the poster, Bill wrote a note to me saying, "Sorry about the last set." *Courtesy of Joe La Barbera.*

tremendous patience and confidence—confidence in his own abilities and the ability he perceived in you.

According to Bill, his experience with Miles Davis was the same: making musical discoveries on his own. As teenagers, my brothers and I spoke with McCoy Tyner on a break when Coltrane's quartet played Rochester, and he confirmed much the same thing about that group. At a point during the tune "Impressions," McCoy stopped playing and we asked him if he got a signal from Coltrane to "stroll" (jazz parlance for stop playing). He said no. He simply couldn't think of anything else to add to the music. Years later Elvin Jones, Coltrane's drummer in that legendary band, told me they never discussed the music beforehand. Even "A Love Supreme" was recorded in this manner with Coltrane passing out untitled parts and counting it off. From what I have read of Cannonball, his group operated on the same basis. Of course, you can rehearse specific parts of an arrangement, but your interpretation of the part is critical to giving a group its identity.

At 18, Andy LaVerne took several piano lessons from Bill Evans at Bill's apartment in the Bronx—just a few blocks away from Andy's home. Bill was extremely generous with his time and did not charge him for the lessons. *Photo by Andy LaVerne. Courtesy of Andy LaVerne.*

For the student who is still learning the basics to the seasoned professional, the "Joy of Discovery" can be a rewarding journey as long as we are all aware of the responsibility that comes with the free rein to explore.

New York-based pianist Andy LaVerne recalls a lesson with Bill ...

I was 18 and had just finished high school when Bill was playing for two weeks at the Village Vanguard. This was the band with Eddie Gomez on bass and Marty Morell on drums. I'd go every night.

Usually at those gigs, Bill would play the set without speaking to the audience. Then he would disappear on the break. It was just fantastic. But on this one night, I was sitting in the front row with my girlfriend. Bill came off the stage and sat down next to our table. He was talking, and I could hear what he was saying. He mentioned that he'd just moved into a new apartment on W. 246th Street in Riverdale, a neighborhood in the Bronx. That was the same street I lived on. Back then, I was very naïve and shy. But I couldn't resist telling him that's where I lived. I went over to the table and said, "Excuse me Mr. Evans ...." and told him that I lived on the same street and also played piano. The next thing you know, he invited me over to his place.

We scheduled a date and time. It was a three-minute walk to his place. He lived in an apartment on the fourth floor but met me in the lobby. Before heading up, he checked his mail where he got a package with a book called *Jazz Improvisation Vol. 4* by John Mehegan.

This book contained all of Bill's left-hand, rootless voicings. At the time (the mid-1960s), I didn't know those yet. It was one of those things that I couldn't figure out at the time. Bill had written the book's introduction.

The upshot is that I took several lessons from Bill, which consisted of me playing for him, while he sat in the upper register of piano. It was kind of nerve wracking. I was going to Julliard at the time, and I didn't know much about jazz theory and harmony. Then he would play for me. I wish he had videos and tapes of those lessons. All I have is the memory, which I hope I can retain.

Then we'd play duets and he spoke to me in conceptual ideas. He said you have to set harmonic goals, and then there's many avenues you can go down to reach that goal. When I looked back over my career and development, that's where I got all that from.

He had a very strong feeling that he didn't want people to play like him. I know that's one of the things he felt very strongly about. He spoke about the "Joy of Discovery."

At the end of the first lesson, he showed me the book he'd just gotten that day. When I was leaving, he said, *Why don't you take this?*

At the time, I didn't really know what was going to happen in terms of paying him, but as it turned out, he never charged me for anything. Nowadays, who doesn't teach? And who teaches for free? Nobody.[2]

Chapter 7

We Will Meet Again
August 1979

Bill was anxious to record the new trio, but there was a wrinkle in the plan. Two previous trio albums—both with drummer Eliot Zigmund and bassist Eddie Gomez—awaited release. One was on Fantasy Records, the other on Warner Bros. The next recording, also slated for Warner Bros., was originally going to feature Bill collaborating with arranger-composer Claus Ogerman and a full orchestra. But Ogerman had a conflict and Bill, wanting to avoid back-to-back trio releases, decided to try something different from his usual format. He opted for a horn-based quintet with the new trio as its nucleus. He was already a big fan of tenor saxophonist Larry Schneider, who had played on *Affinity*, Bill's 1979 album that also featured Toots Thielemans on harmonica. When he asked me if I had any preference for trumpet, I recommended Tom Harrell, with whom I'd been playing a lot of late.

We recorded at CBS' 30th Street Studio in Manhattan. Owned by Columbia Records, the studio was a vast 10,000-square foot former church that was left virtually intact to preserve the glorious acoustics and was widely considered among the best of its era.[1] All the greats in jazz had recorded here including Louis Armstrong, Miles Davis, Dave Brubeck and Duke Ellington.[2] To say the least, I was excited. I had recorded before, but this was with Bill Evans. Going on record with Bill was a big deal for me, and I was there to play. I wanted it to be right. It was also a big deal to record in this hallowed hall where countless Miles Davis sessions had previously been recorded. The history was literally oozing from the walls!

The session took place over four days from August 6 to 9. The mood was very upbeat and positive. Miles Davis famously recorded *Kind of Blue* and many of his studio sessions like *Porgy and Bess* and *Sketches of Spain* at this studio. Larry and Tom asked Bill where Miles and John Coltrane stood during the *Kind of Blue* session and adopted those positions. The band's footprint covered as much space as my living room with the piano not more than 10 feet from me. There was probably a half baffle between my drums and the other musicians. Also, at Bill's request, we didn't use headphones. This really forced us to listen and still get the right sound. I'd have to say I thought it came out really well. Much of the credit goes to the engineer Frank Laico, who'd handled the same chores for Miles Davis' *Milestones* album, Tony Bennett, Thelonious Monk and numerous Broadway recordings. Frank and I became friends from that day on and we would work again on sessions for Tony Bennett.[3]

We didn't rehearse for the session. Bill did it the way they always used to do it. The music was there when we showed up. We ran down a head and talked about who would solo before the tape rolled. And then we started. We recorded two takes for every tune except one: "Bill's Hit Tune." We must have done a dozen takes on that one. Bill was not happy with something, possibly because the horns played it exactly as written, and he may have wanted more rhythmic liberty with the phrasing. This was something that most jazz musicians will do once they are completely comfortable with the melody, but it's impossible for two horns to do this without some guidance or at least some time playing it together.

Helen Keane, Bill's longtime manager, produced the session, as she did with nearly all of his recording dates. Helen was a striking presence—tall, blond and imposing. My first impression was that of a total professional, which proved to be true. She was also personable once you got to know her, but she was tough as nails when need be. And she was obviously totally devoted to Bill and his career.

Helen started her career as the first woman agent at MCA, a powerhouse talent agency, booking musicians and eventually branching out to television, film and radio. In getting that job, she broke a glass ceiling, giving women the option or at least the possibility of becoming full-fledged agents. In time, she would represent Kenny Burrell, Art Farmer, Joanne Brackeen, actor Geoffrey Holder (best known for his 7-Up "Un-Cola" television ads) and renowned dancer/choreographer Carmen de Lavallade. But Bill was her No. 1 client. At times, her other jazz acts secured jobs because it could also mean eventually booking Bill. Serving as Bill's personal manager and producer seemed logical. She knew all of Bill's habits and preferences for recording. She knew the recording environment he liked and what specifics he needed to feel comfortable—as opposed to an attitude of, "I'll book a studio and you just show up." Bill and Helen had a handshake agreement that lasted over 25 years and Bill always had complete confidence in her judgment regarding labels, recording, booking, all of it really. On the night her then-husband Gene Lees brought her to the Village Vanguard to hear Bill for the first time as a possible client, she said, "Oh no, this one is going to break my heart." That turned out to be true on more than one occasion, but, regardless, she protected him with a fierce and vigilant fervor. Without doubt she was the ideal manager for Bill.

In all, we recorded seven of Bill's original tunes and one standard, "For All We Know." A few were pretty challenging. "Comrade Conrad" is divided into two sections, one in 4/4 time and the second in 3/4 (waltz) time, toggling back and forth over the course of the song. But during the soloing, the melody instruments change key signatures for each chorus, and this is where Larry and Tom's experience came through because they did this on the fly! "Five" was a rhythmic workout with the melody line often playing five notes in the space of four beats to the measure. None of this was exactly easy sight-reading material for the horns. Marc and I had been playing this periodically with Bill on the gig so we were fairly comfortable with it.

My personal favorite track from this session is "For All We Know," written in 1934 and previously recorded by Billie Holiday, among others.

Bill was attracted to the song from a recording done by Roberta Flack and Donny Hathaway, a very powerful and almost prophetic performance. Donny committed suicide on January 13, 1979, a fact that did not go unnoticed by Bill who once commented on this to me, implying that, perhaps, Donny had decided he had had enough of this life. (Most Bill Evans fans will probably be surprised to learn that Bill was sometimes moved by and impressed with vocal music outside of what we normally think of as jazz. An example of this was Bill's near nightly performance of "Mornin' Glory" by Bobbie Gentry. The musical range of Bill Evans never ceased to amaze and surprise.)

Bassist Marc Johnson recalled that session ...

Because I had recorded with Bill in the studio the year before, I knew a little more about what to expect from him—that there would be multiple takes as he worked out formats and went over the tunes with the musicians. I knew Larry Schneider from the *Affinity* album date with Bill and Toots Thielemans, but I only knew Tom Harrell a little by reputation.

We had already been playing some of the tunes either on the gig or at sound checks, so we were familiar with "Bill's Hit Tune," "Five" and "Laurie." We had played "Five" as sort of a closer after the third set at the Village Vanguard. I was familiar with "Comrade Conrad" from hearing it on a previous Bill Evans album ... same with "Peri's Scope." I didn't know "Only Child."

Helen Keane left the music up to Bill. She gave an opinion about the relative merits of certain takes, and she handled the nuts and bolts of making a recording session happen. But in all things musical, she deferred to Bill.

I do recall that Tom Harrell would retreat to the bathroom a lot, and Bill would have to go get him before almost every take. It wasn't until much later that I learned that Tom suffered from schizophrenia. He plays so beautifully in spite of it.

I felt lucky to be a part of any music Bill was making and just wanted to play well for Bill and Joe and the band.[4]

I didn't know "Only Child" either but was attracted immediately to the melody. Tom and Larry may not recall this but I remember Bill tasking them with creating the coda to this tune. It was really an example of Bill being a mentor because he was offering them an opportunity to be involved on another level in the production process. He said something to the effect of *You guys come up with an ending while I go out for a smoke.* When he returned about twenty minutes later, we still didn't have an ending, so Bill walked over to the piano and said to everyone, "Write this down," and proceeded to spontaneously compose the ending, which we used on the recording, and it's a beauty!

The sessions paid double scale, so we made a nice taste. At the 23rd Annual Grammy Awards in 1980, the album took the award for "Best Jazz Instrumental Performance, Group." Bill also won for "Best Jazz Instrumental Performance, Soloist" for "I Will Say Goodbye."[5] Bill picked up the Grammy at a ceremony in New York (and I vaguely recall attending). The website allmusic.com rated it four (out of five) stars.[6]

Chapter 8

Hanging with Bill 1

After my wife got pregnant, we moved upstate to a little suburb of Kingston, New York, called Lake Katrine, about two and a half hours from Manhattan. Whenever I had work in the city, with or without Bill, he let me stay at his apartment in Fort Lee, New Jersey, which reduced commute time and expenses. Perhaps more significantly, this also allowed me the opportunity to get to know Bill a little better because when we were on the road—with the exception of the show—Bill was not to be seen. I think it was "Philly" Joe Jones who nicknamed him "The Phantom"—and for good reason.

One such occasion happened the last two weeks of February 1980. I was hired to work at Michael's Pub with Jimmy Rowles, Carol Sloane and George Mraz, so naturally I stayed with Bill. During the day, he would occasionally come out of his bedroom, and we would talk about various things: music, life, something we may have watched on T.V. the night before. I figured since I was staying there, I would cook to save money and asked him what he liked to eat. He had two ready responses: tortellini Bolognese and hot dogs! Period! Over the course of my visits, I made the pasta, hot dogs and breakfast, and I cannot tell you how happy I made this man with such a simple offering.

I think he really just appreciated the kind gesture because, let's face it, it was just hot dogs or eggs.

Bill and his wife Nenette had separated several months earlier and one day he went to visit her and their son, Evan, in New Haven. Things didn't go well. I had gone out for a while, and when I got back, Bill was waiting for me in the entryway and literally broke down crying. My response was the only humane thing I could think of: I took him in my arms. This was one of three times that I helped Bill by physically holding him and, of the three, it was by far the least difficult. He eventually calmed down and we sat and talked for a while. He had brought back a box of his belongings that included a treasure trove of items, among them some recordings he had made in high school and college. We spent the afternoon listening to these, and Bill let me copy what I wanted.

There was a certain hominess to Bill's place, especially in the music area. There was a TV in the living room as well as Bill's wonderful old, 5-foot Chickering baby grand piano, on which sat new sheet music from the likes of Johnny Mandel and Marilyn and Alan Bergman. One day when I thought Bill had fallen asleep, I quietly played the piano, more than likely something of his that I had learned. I probably played for all of five minutes and then stopped. From the bedroom I heard Bill say, "Keep playing." I couldn't believe it because I am a rotten piano player. But for some reason, he wanted to hear more, so I played pretty much everything I could think of and even gave Mandel's tune a shot (it was something called "Melt Away" that I don't think ever saw the light of day). Later, Bill came out and complimented me. Then he sat down and showed me some things at the keyboard, like his arrangement of "Our Delight." I'm sure I was the envy of every real piano player in the world that day.

Other than my lame piano playing, there was rarely music on in the apartment. Bill preferred listening to talk radio, political or otherwise, or watching television. And, speaking of politics, there is one event that comes to mind. The trio was scheduled to play five concerts in Moscow in September of 1980, and Bill was looking forward to it. His mother's family, Saroka, hailed from Russia, and his father was of Welsh descent. Both family cultures embraced music and, in particular, singing. This was Bill's first introduction to music.

There was also every indication that he had a strong following in his maternal homeland. When Russia invaded Afghanistan in 1979, Bill felt compelled to respond. In a letter to the editor of *DownBeat* (published a month after he passed), Bill publicly canceled the trip and hoped his letter would reach his target audience of fans here and in Russia. Here is an excerpt from that letter:

"My name, Evans, is obviously Welsh but my mother's name, Saroka, and heritage is Russian. Memories of my childhood are warmly crowded with the singing and spirit of this heritage … a priceless gift of enrichment to a growing child. Consequently, I have always hoped to visit Russia, to feel at first hand the roots of this part of myself. Perhaps even without the catalyst of Afghanistan, I might have arrived at the following conclusion for I had often lamented the tragedy of people living in a society where one's opinion could bring about long suffering, imprisonment, and where an artist's purest inspiration was expected to conform to outside criteria. The very denial of the essence of art today! To perform there voluntarily, after all, is to walk passively in the atmosphere of the degradation of the human spirit. My gesture will have little or no significance, but I follow my code and am at peace with myself."[1]

I follow my code and am at peace with myself. This closing statement, for better or worse, summarizes Bill's entire life.

Chapter 9

Birthday Blues
and Buenos Aires
August–September 1979

Bill's 50th birthday was rapidly approaching. The big day was August 16, and Garry Dial, a wonderful pianist who worked with Red Rodney-Ira Sullivan band, offered to host a party. Garry lived at Manhattan Plaza, two high-rise towers at W. 43rd St. built by New York City in the mid-1970s. By law, some 70 percent of the tenants worked in performing arts (including Charles Mingus).[1] Garry's pad had a pretty hip view. In a state of youthful, sophomoric humor, Marc and I found an erotic bakery on the Upper East Side. We ordered a birthday cake with a suggestive message. Bill got a chuckle out of it.

A number of great musicians showed up, including Kenny Werner, Joanne Brackeen and Joe Lovano. So did Bill's estranged wife Nenette. It was a happy event. Bill was in pretty good spirits and still pretty healthy then. He and Nenette—though separated—were still getting along pretty well. Bill played solo piano for a bit, and then Joanne played some duets with him, which we all enjoyed very much.

When Joanne joined Bill, he opted to play at the low end of the piano, supplying a bass line and comping (improvising with chords to support soloing).

Garry Dial recalled the party ...

I was actually playing with Marc Johnson during those years before he got the gig with Bill and also while he played with him. Marc used to come over to my apartment at Manhattan Plaza, and we would play tunes. So when he came over to my pad to play, he really liked the apartment. I live on the 44th floor, and it's a ridiculous view and a nice scene to play. Looking south back then, you could see midtown, the Empire State building, Times Square and all of New Jersey (since then, a skyscraper has taken out the south view).

Marc brought up the idea, saying, "Wow, man, maybe we should have Bill's birthday party here?" And I said, "Fine with me." I jumped at the chance. But it was really Marc's idea, thinking that Bill would dig the pad and the view, the whole scene.

We invited all our friends. There were about 30 guests, including Kenny Werner, Joe Lovano, bassist Frank Gravis, trumpeter Greg Ruvolo (who took a photo of me and Bill), pianists Joanne Brackeen and Gerard D'Angelo, drummer Jeff Hirshfield and Bill's wife, Nenette. I had the party catered with some sandwiches, hors d'oeuvres, wine and mixed drinks.

We were all just kind of sitting around chatting before he got there. I had the piano, a 6-foot Yamaha conservatory model, tuned and voiced. And I had microphones in it set for his touch. I wouldn't have forced him to play, but I thought if he wanted to, the piano was ready to go.

Bill was very nice and clearly glad to be there. When he arrived, I had a recording of Bill playing "Waltz for Debby" with Cannonball Adderley playing on the stereo. And Bill said, "Wow, I haven't heard that record since I did it. I don't have it. I never heard it." And he went over to the piano and sat down and started to play along with it. So immediately, when he sat down, I turned the record off and said, "Bill, would you mind if I recorded you?" And he looked up and was really cool about it, and said, "Sure, man." It was just really fun.

I'll never forget standing on one side of the piano and watching him play like that, and Marc Johnson was on the other side of the piano, saying, "Hey, Bill, play "Fun Ride." And Bill was taking requests. Not from me, but he did from Marc.

He played solo piano for about 25 or 30 minutes. Besides "Fun Ride" he played "Laurie," "For All We Know," "Bill's Hit Tune," and "Letter to Evan." Bill played about 35 minutes, joking around between tunes. Then he invited Joanne Brackeen to play a duet with him. Helen Keane was going to manage Joanne, too, so Bill wanted to hear her. They played "Freddie Freeloader" and "Speak Low." Then Joanne played a tune by herself. Then came the birthday cake. Kenny Werner played "Happy Birthday" on the piano. After the cake was served, Bill left but everybody else stayed. Then Kenny played some solo piano, and I played a duet with Gerard D'Angelo.

One amusing thing that happened was I got to confirm a wild story I'd heard about Bill's playing. In those days, Red Rodney came over to my apartment almost five days a week while I played in his band. During one such visit, I mentioned that I was going to host Bill's birthday party. He said, "When we were in Oscar Pettiford's band, Oscar hated Bill's comping so much, he took an axe off the wall and threatened to kill him." I insisted the story was bullshit. But Red said to me, "Don't comp like Bill."

Yet Bill confirmed the story to me that night at the birthday party. "I ran off the bandstand, and Oscar came after me with an axe," Bill said. "I didn't really know what it was about but heard it had to do with my comping."

I first got into Bill when I was in high school, hearing him at the Top of the Gate with drummer Marty Morell and bassist Eddie Gomez, a large club at the intersection of Thompson and Bleecker streets. A few years later, I played with bassist Chuck Israels and, while I was a student at Berklee College of Music, with drummer Joe Hunt, both alumni of Bill's bands. Joe was on Berklee's faculty at the time. So I learned more about Bill from that experience.

When Marc and Joe got on the gig, it was such a great feeling for all of us because Bill was now playing with our peer group.

> Hearing them play "Nardis" tells the whole story of the "last trio." Bill played a long, open extended solo to start the tune, but he transcended himself. He was getting more into polytonal chords and more displaced rhythmic stuff. Then Marc would play a solo. Then Joe would play a solo. Then Bill would come in and they'd play together. It's amazing to study the development of that tune for the history of the trio. Bill called it the therapy tune because they'd play it at the end of the evening and just let everything go.[2]

After reading Garry's recollection of Oscar Pettiford's reaction to Bill's comping: Well, I guess not everybody dug Bill Evans!

In September 1979, the trio traveled to South America with numerous dates in Brazil and Argentina. It was a really wonderful experience in many ways. First of all, the fans in both countries were tremendous in their appreciation of Bill and the trio and also in their generosity.

Pianist Garry Dial hosted a 50th birthday party for Bill. Many of New York's finest jazz musicians, including Joanne Brackeen, Joe Lovano and Kenny Werner, attended the affair at Dial's apartment in Manhattan Plaza. *Photo by Greg Ruvolo. Courtesy of Garry Dial.*

We were treated to some great food, sometimes in unusual settings. In Buenos Aires, we traveled on a long boat ride through a series of canals that got narrower until we were seemingly in the middle of nowhere. But then, suddenly, a restaurant appeared where we enjoyed a fabulous seafood lunch.

I remember that the concerts were mostly in theaters because many fans showed up with cassette players, and Helen marched up and down the front of the stage every night removing them.

We also took in a show at Caño 14, a tango club in Buenos Aires, which turned out to be quite an experience. The band was led by bandoneon master Walter Rios and consisted of several bandoneon players and a series of vocalists, both male and female. As it turns out, the singers were arranged in order of their status or ability. To my ears, the very first singer was great but with each successive artist, the level rose until the very last one, who brought the house down with an emotionally charged performance. This vocalist was so unbelievable that we had tears in our eyes. We didn't understand a word this person sang, but the music was just astounding. Unforgettable. After the concert Bill congratulated Rios, who was amazed to see his hero in attendance. The following evening Walter Rios and legendary tango composer Astor Piazzolla came to hear the trio and were greeted warmly by Bill.

While in Rio, we visited Luis Eça, at a small, local supper club, Chiko's Bar, an intimate listening room facing Ipanema Beach, where Luis played a solo gig. Luis composed "The Dolphin," a jazz classic, and was an old friend of Bill's. To the delight of the audience, Bill and Marc sat in. Unfortunately, for me there were no drums. The place went crazy.

In Brazil, we also played in São Paulo and Brasilia. Fans and old friends flew in from remote areas in order to visit Bill and attend a concert. I remember the concert in Brasilia because the operator of the theater we performed at had misgivings about allowing a jazz pianist access to their top concert piano. Bill was not satisfied with the instrument they provided and stressed the importance of a good piano for a good performance. I don't remember if he got the good piano or not. But I do remember Bill going to their piano storage room, where he found several superior instruments.

I also remember swimming at Ipanema Beach. At the time they still discharged raw waste into the bay there. Locals were used to it, but if you're coming from outside the area you're not, so I got pretty sick.

It was while we were in Rio that I did a very bad thing to a very good person … namely, Marc Johnson. For some time now Marc and I had been watching Bill's drug use increase as his health diminished and, at times, his playing suffered. Marc asked me what the fascination was with cocaine. I had used it on occasion myself but never had the money or desire to have a serious habit. I saw this as an opportunity to show Bill how his behavior was influencing Marc, who Bill described as a "pure spirit."

So I called Bill in his hotel room and said that Marc wanted to try cocaine and that Bill should supply it. We went to Bill's room, and he was shooting daggers at me but gave us enough for Marc to try some, all the while preaching about its ill effects. Well, we tried it and Marc decided (thank goodness) that it was no big deal; that was the end of it.

Later, Bill called me and told me to never do anything like that again to Marc. I told him that his example caused the problem and that if he wanted to protect Marc, he should stop. OK, total bush-league psychology on my part and also being a bit of an asshole, but I was willing to try anything at this point to get Bill to change his ways, even a little bit. How naïve!

Chapter 10

Hanging with Bill 2

A t Bill's apartment, our conversations over meals ran the gamut from the music to the mundane. During one of these talks, we spoke about the iconic Miles Davis recording *Kind of Blue,* and I was stunned to hear Bill refer to it as *just another record date.* He wasn't downplaying what was ultimately accomplished that day but merely stating the obviously high level of commitment that great jazz musicians bring to every session.

In one of his final recorded interviews with Ross Porter, Bill acknowledged the importance of this monumental recording. "I often wondered why it had penetrated so much and been such an influence," he said. "And it was only recently that I was returning from the Village Vanguard in my car and happened to turn on the radio and "All Blues" was just starting ... And somehow I had gotten a little more objective insight into it and I realized that there was some kind of special thing happening."[1]

On one occasion, I asked about the trio with bassist Scott LaFaro and drummer Paul Motian, who were both, of course, very special to Bill. Paul and Bill had hooked up early in their careers playing in bands led by clarinetists Tony Scott and Jerry Wald. Later, Bill hired Paul for his very first recording as a leader, *New Jazz Conceptions,* released in 1957 on Riverside

Records. I regret never having had the opportunity to speak with Paul at length, but I did get to say hello one night when he came to the Vanguard. Apparently, he asked Bill to do a reunion trio recording with himself and a bass player, but Bill declined.

Scott LaFaro was indeed very special to Bill on more than just a musical level. I told Bill how much of an influence Scott had been to me and the fact that he was from Geneva, New York, which was not too far away from my hometown of Mt. Morris. I also recalled seeing Scott's obituary in *DownBeat* shortly after he was killed in a car accident. This is when Bill told me about getting Scott's winter coat from his girlfriend, Gloria. Bill said he wore it until it literally fell apart. After this conversation, Bill gave me one of his shirts, which I have to this day but have never worn.

On another occasion, I mentioned a highly successful musician in town who could really play jazz but opted for a career in the studios. In my opinion, it was a loss, but Bill simply said that "he made that choice." Bill reiterated that comment in a radio interview with deejay Dick Buckley in Chicago about another well-known pianist.[2] These observations were not a criticism—simply a statement of fact without judgment.

Bill often also said that "talent is cheap." In an interview with Georgia Urban, writing for *The Entertainer* in Schenectady, New York, Bill went further. "Even your local milkman probably has a great talent," he told her (no disrespect to those dedicated folks!). "It requires a lot of other qualities along with ability such as accepting the realities of this business, being able to handle yourself professionally and never allowing your personal life to infringe on your professional self. And if you're truly an artist, you will not be preoccupied with ego things."[3]

What was of the utmost importance for Bill was the willingness to commit to your art and stay with it. Let's face it, Bill Evans could have done most anything in music he chose to, including studio work.

"I gave myself provisionally until I was 30," he told Porter. "I came here when I was 25, and I said I'm going to just completely dedicate myself for five years, and if I haven't made a decent dent, if I don't get the kind of response in five years that shows me that what I think I can do, the world thinks I can do also, then I'll have to make another choice. Become somebody's musical director or go into the studios or whatever. So, I did that and it opened up really nicely, and I think a lot of being successful at what you want to do has to do with keeping your focus, not being detoured and hanging in there."[4]

In the previous interview with Georgia Urban, Bill spoke about being approached by singer Tony Martin in 1955 when he first arrived in New York. The job would pay $25,000 a year for an 18-week commitment— big money in those days, for sure! "It took me all of ten seconds to turn it down," Bill said, knowing that it would ultimately sidetrack his real ambition to be a jazz musician.[5] This reflected Bill's ironclad sense of commitment to the art form. Bill possessed all the necessary skills to literally do anything in music—from musical director to session work (his sight-reading ability was legendary). But his commitment to jazz was final, and he would give everything to it.

Chapter 11

Expectations

rtists constantly place high demands on themselves in the pursuit of their craft yet often feel frustrated when they don't reach that level every time. Such expectations are unrealistic, but, nonetheless, they persist over time. For me, such frustrations could sometimes seem commonplace. Bill operated on a much higher level and rarely let these things bother him. He was human, and from time to time, he would voice frustration with a performance. But largely, he had a more sensible approach to performance that I guess came from years of experience and a true confidence in himself. In the video he made with his brother Harry, *The Universal Mind of Bill Evans: The Creative Process and Self Teaching*, Bill spoke of training yourself to focus all your attention when needed.[1] He used the phrase "flicking a switch" to describe how he initiated the process. And in the two years I worked with him, he never seemed less than 100 percent immersed in the music whenever we played. Of course, there were times when it seemed like more of a struggle to get things rolling. At times like these, Bill resorted to what he called playing "your professional best." That may sound like a mundane and workmanlike approach to art, but it never diminished the quality of the playing and opened the way to what we strived for in the first place.

We all have recordings that we value above all others and possibly life changing in their impact. *Jazz Track*, *Kind of Blue* and *Waltz for Debby* all fit into this category for me. But it can become a problem when you find yourself performing with the artist from one of your favorites, and the *magic* doesn't appear every night. Which brings me back to my own unrealistic expectations playing every night with Bill. Such moments appeared early on. Usually it had to do with the acoustics, not being able to hear what I needed or not getting my sound in a venue. At one point, Bill must have sensed my frustration because he took me aside for a talk. He patiently explained that it would be impossible to achieve the highest level of performance night after night but assured me the quality would never drop below a high professional level. In fact, it would always be very good and, perhaps most important, please the audience. That all made sense, but it was easier said than done for me. It would actually take longer than my time with Bill to feel comfortable with my performance and accept the outcome on a particular night; but, in time, I got there.

Other expectations also surfaced. I expected this group to stay together for a while and grow musically. Bill's popularity was peaking, and the trio was attracting attention, so it seemed getting work would not be a problem. We were scheduled to tour Japan in October 1980 and there was talk of an Australian tour as well. Musically, we were reaching a high level of communication within the trio and with the audience. So all prospects for the future seemed good except for one thing: Bill's health.

I had known of Bill's history of substance abuse since reading about it in high school. When I joined the band, his prior addiction was common knowledge, but it was also known that he was in a methadone treatment program at Rockefeller Hospital.[2] Sometime before I'd joined, Bill had begun using again. And after about a year with the trio, I'd begun noticing that it was affecting the music.

When I first started playing with Bill, the groove was rock solid, the tempos firm. Playing Bill's music involved a detailed interplay among all three instruments, an innovative, contrapuntal approach to piano trio. All three instruments improvised off one another's musical statements. Sometimes a piano motif might provoke a drum fill, which, in turn, might inspire Marc to embellish his "walking" bass line. At times, Marc and I would just lay down as exciting and swinging a groove as possible, a pad for Bill's exemplary soloing. And Bill broke new ground by playing ideas and then restating them but in different places in the meter. Executing this kind of playing was akin to walking a tightrope without a net, mainly because everyone had to hear the music's basic time pulse in the exact same place. When I joined the band, I could play and express anything I wanted to without any concern about that pulse. I was confident that when my sticks landed, Bill would be in the same place even when he wasn't saying something that second. Marc, too.

But after Bill's brother, Harry, committed suicide, it seemed like that changed. Bill's tempos began to rush, at times, badly. Marc and I noticed the trend and privately wondered on breaks and after shows if drugs played a role. I raised the question to Bill at lunch during a week-long stay in Tucson doing workshops and clinics. It was the first time we spoke of his drug use because I'd seen him snorting coke earlier. So I asked him if he thought it affected the music—which was my not-so-subtle way of saying, "It's affecting the music."

That was the first time we talked about the drug thing and then, of course, we had other conversations along the way. After returning from Europe, we played at Lulu White's in Boston the following October. And on the break, Bill and I came to verbal blows over his rushing. By then, I'd raised the topic with him a few times. I can't recall word-for-word what was said, but it was something like, *Bill, are you aware how much the tempos are picking up?* I was trying to convey that playing drums was becoming difficult when he rushed a line. Well, he blew up at me. He went ballistic and said, "Just deal with it." He was very terse, very belligerent, but I think it was borne out of frustration because he couldn't control it. I make this observation with the benefit of 20–20 hindsight.

Some of these problems leaked onto recordings and didn't go unnoticed by reviewers or biographers. Laurie Verchomin, who'd assumed the job of looking after Bill, was doing remarkably well under these circumstances. For such a young woman (23 at the time), she dealt more and more with Bill's health on a daily basis—no small task. Through all this, Bill adamantly refused serious medical counsel. He cheated often on his regimen in the methadone program either by not taking his proper dosage or by returning to cocaine and that also caused problems. On a few occasions, I spoke to the doctor there on Bill's behalf. As often as not, the physician gave me a pep talk to try and keep Bill in line—which was preposterous. Bill was very intelligent and could see through any attempts on my part at manipulating his behavior. After reading Laurie's account of this period in her book, *The Big Love: Life and Death with Bill Evans*, I think her expectations were to be there for Bill to the end.

As frustrating as this was, I must emphasize that I believe Bill's drug use affected his craft, not his content. Bill's ideas, melodies, harmonic vocabulary never changed. He always seemed able to "flick the switch" and give 100 percent on every gig. Bill still played at the highest level imaginable among his peers back then.

I snorted some "blow" with Bill from time to time and even drove him to score once in a bad area of Manhattan. But I was never seriously using it that much. For one thing, it wreaked havoc with my sinuses. For another, I couldn't afford it. And then when my daughter was born on February 29, 1980, I considered the reality of feeding another mouth and the expenses involved. I just said, *that's the end of it.*

That all said, Bill's drug use began eroding my long-term expectations for the band. I was willing to dedicate myself to this trio and make sacrifices (traveling and being away from my family). I was looking for a future with it, reaching a point where the trio hopefully broke new ground in jazz and—while no one expects to get rich playing this music—reaching some financial stability (the Modern Jazz Quartet came to mind at the time, but obviously our trio was not a cooperative). But this required another critical expectation: that Bill would live, allowing the band to thrive and not burn out in a year or two.

Providing for my family back home also added to my frustration. Despite prospective bookings overseas and about a half-dozen week-long stints a year at the Village Vanguard (and other similar major clubs around the country), work appeared to be slowing down.

To make ends meet, I'd work with anyone in New York who called for club dates. Marc and I did some recordings at a studio at Yale University with trumpeter Tom Harrell, saxophonist Jerry Bergonzi and pianist Andy LaVerne. And I did some recordings with singer Carol Sloane and pianist Jimmy Rowles. But I also worked with a great wedding band based near my home in upstate New York. The group featured accordion and tenor sax—and they were great players. We played polkas and other typical wedding fare for gigs in the Hudson Valley between Nyack and Kingston. I found it ironic that I was doing this while working with Bill as he did the same thing when he first arrived in New York. He always had his tuxedo pressed and ready to go if a call for a gig came in. For me, it was an experience I'd known since childhood. I knew the drill from the time I was six or seven years old.

So with Bill's gigs slowing down, I brought it up to Helen Keane, who tersely said, "Talk to your boss." Helen and I argued about this but managed to get past it. In fact, she and I enjoyed a very good relationship for many years until her death in 1996. The sober reality: Bill's health was now jeopardizing his ability to take more gigs, and I'm sure that Helen was as frustrated by this situation as anyone. It was a double-edged sword: Bill needed money to live but didn't have the strength to tour at a pace where the trio could make a comfortable living. At one point, I thought I should just cut my losses and walk away, but I couldn't bring myself to do it.

If you compare Bill physically from the Ames, Iowa, broadcast to the final video from Molde, Norway, the difference is striking—even though his playing was as strong as ever. In spite of his obvious physical deterioration at the Molde concert, Bill played piano with the vigor of a weightlifter bench pressing 250 pounds. When I joined the band, he seemed a lot more robust. Yet, in reality, by this time, he was gaunt, pale and thin. If I had really been watching him more than listening to his playing, I would have noticed how much he'd withered away physically. If you need a visible comparison just look at the covers of the albums he did with Tony Bennett where he is easily 20 pounds heavier. I didn't notice that until the very end. Recently I attended a 90th birthday party for a friend and saw many folks

I had not seen in over a year. The physical change to all of us was striking because of the amount of time between seeing each other. By contrast, I saw Bill almost daily, so it's understandable why I didn't notice his physical decline much more.

Reading these words today makes me feel selfish and ashamed, but that is today's reality. The reality I was facing in 1980 was completely different.

Chapter 12

Hanging with Bill 3

Musicians' humor is an acquired taste. Whenever I would return home from a tour in recent years, my wife, Gillian, would always jokingly say to me, "OK, let's hear them all now and get this out of the way," a reference to the numerous jokes I would bring home. Admittedly, some were not that great. Or maybe it's my delivery?

One morning at Bill's over breakfast, we talked about an episode of *The Mary Tyler Moore Show* that we had both watched separately the prior evening and found hilarious. In this particular show, Lou Grant (Ed Asner) consoled Mary after yet another failed relationship. As he cradles her in his arms, he sings the verse to an old Irish lullaby, "Too Ra Loo Ra Loo Ral":

Over In Killarney, Many Years Ago
My Mother Sang A Song To Me In Tones So Soft And Low
Just A Simple Little Ditty In Her Good Old Irish Way
And I'd Give The World If I Could Hear That Song Of Hers Today.

But when he gets to the chorus, he breaks into "Up the Lazy River"! It still cracked us up the next morning. As I said … musicians' humor.

***

Most days, Bill lay in bed a lot. But on occasion, when feeling stronger, he would make his way from the bedroom into the living room and play some of the sheet music sent to him by friends like Johnny Mandel. He was also working on new tunes like "Knit For Mary F," which I distinctly remember. He showed me the intro he used on "Our Delight" and a few other things which I can't remember now. He rarely had music playing in the apartment except the day he returned from New Haven with all the early recordings of himself in high school, college and beyond. Many of these were cardboard discs (an inexpensive recording technology from the 1940s). We listened to a lot of it. and I was completely fascinated. The genesis of a genius. He let me copy what I wanted onto a cassette which I still have today.

***

Bill was quite an athlete in his youth playing golf, tennis, bowling and football. Tennis legend Don Budge was a fan of Bill's, but I don't know if they ever played together. I have heard that Bill was an excellent golfer, but he didn't speak of it and certainly never went to play a round during my time with him. His physical condition would not have allowed it. He did talk about the golf driving range that his family operated and where he would help out. He loved the track (horse racing) and would often go with friends like Joe Puma to see the trotters in nearby Yonkers. I once heard Bill recount his betting system at the track to a Chicago radio host. What followed was an informed, analytical and comprehensive approach that would more often than not net winning results. Things like knowing the track, the daily conditions, the jockeys, the horses, how many races each had run that week and so on. In Bill's opinion, you could enjoy it as an art without betting and that it was like listening to a great piece of music unfold. My first wife, Carole, and I went with Bill to Yonkers Raceway one fateful evening and surrendered $50.00 which we could ill afford by picking horses' names we liked. Bill, not surprisingly, came away a winner.

Backstage at a club somewhere, Bill demonstrated yet another hidden athletic skill: pool. I had played a bit in my youth and thought I was pretty good, but he easily cleaned house on me. There's always a bit more than meets the eye, I guess.

Chapter 13

The Paris Concert—
Europe 1979
November 16 to December 13

In November, the trio ventured across the Atlantic for the first of two visits to Europe. The tour started in the Netherlands on November 16, where we shared a double bill with tenor saxophonist Stan Getz. His quartet would pair up with us on a few other gigs later in the tour. On yet another show date (also in the Netherlands), Toots Thielemans joined us.

From the Netherlands, the trio flew to Italy and performed at Teatro Morlacchi in Perugia, where I bought a few boxes of my favorite chocolates—one of this region's best known treats. I got these for my family, but it's doubtful they made it all the way through the tour.

From there, we flew to Paris, and I remember waking up the next day on the top floor of a lovely boutique hotel with a little balcony. Nothing extravagant, but it was a beautiful morning, birds were singing, and the rest of the day unfolded much the same because the concert was spectacular.

The date was November 26, 1979, and we performed two sold-out shows that night at the L'Espace Cardin, a 600-plus-seat theater that opened in the early 1930s.[1] French radio recorded both sets for a one-time broadcast. Warner Bros. later decided to release the two sets separately on its subsidiary, Elektra Records, as *The Paris Concert Edition 1* and *The Paris Concert*

A poster for the trio's performance in Perugia, Italy. I painstakingly removed this poster from a wall and preserved it for the rest of the tour. *Courtesy of Joe La Barbera.*

Edition 2. (By now, we were fresh on the heels of Ames, Iowa, the Pacific Northwest tour and all those dates where the trio started to get a feel and gel pretty well.) That night in Paris was effortless. Bill was on, and the audiences just loved it. The kind of energy you get from a full house like that is just unbelievable. It spurs you on. So we felt good, and everything sounded good. My calf drum heads stayed in tune (calf heads are highly susceptible

Bill Evans during sound check for the famed concert at L'Espace Cardin on November 26, 1979. Both sets were recorded for release later on Elektra Records. I wish everyone could have experienced Bill's delight with this piano. *Courtesy of François Lacharme.*

Marc Johnson and me during sound check at L'Espace Cardin. This would turn out to be one of the most memorable evenings the trio ever experienced. *Courtesy of François Lacharme.*

to changes in the weather but offer a tone I prefer more than plastic heads). It was all systems are "go."

There were no set-lists. Like Count Basie, Bill started every tune at the piano and set the tempo accordingly. Our chemistry was so firm that when Bill merely laid his hands on the piano and voiced a chord, we knew the song and where he was headed. Bill's book was now 50-plus tunes strong, and he could pull anything he wanted. We played tunes that night that just seemed to reach the peak you wanted them to reach. My favorite moments were the two solo piano pieces, "I Loves You, Porgy" and "Noelle's Theme." Bill was so inspired by the gorgeous sound of the piano that the performance brought a feeling of transcendence to the hall.

For certain periods of Bill's career, some tunes came up more than others. During this tour, we played "Beautiful Love" (a first for this trio) as well as "Re: Person I Knew" and "All Mine (Minha)." We also performed "Nardis" featuring the whole trio. Throughout his career, Bill played this so often and so well that many have assumed he composed it despite his consistent denial of authorship. Bill also called "34 Skidoo," which I didn't solo on but recall an intense and wonderful interaction. I don't think we did Dave Brubeck's "In Your Own Sweet Way," but tunes would come and go as needed when Bill would be looking for a certain energy. Maybe at a certain point in a set, if he didn't call "Beautiful Love," he might call up "In Your Own Sweet Way" because the tempos are similar. Both are features for the drums, where we trade solos in chorus, eight- and four-bar groupings.

After the show, there was a nice hang backstage. Many longtime fans and friends came to chat with Bill. Drummer Kenny "Klook" Clarke, an American expatriate living in Paris, was among the guests. For those readers who are not aware of Kenny and his important contributions to modern jazz drumming, suffice it to say that he forever changed the way the drums would perform in a jazz band, including playing accompaniment and soloing. Klook came over and said hello. I told him he'd been a hero of mine since the release of *The Birdland Stars on Tour 1956 Presents: The East-West Jazz Septet*, an album we had as kids. (I later learned that on that recording and many others Klook only used a snare drum, bass drum, hi-hat and ride cymbal. With that setup, he emphasized melodic ideas—which I was hearing, too. Much later *Tonight Show* drummer Ed Shaughnessy told me that Kenny would only bring tom-toms to a record date if it paid double scale!) The guy had done it all, so it was great meeting him. He said he liked what I was doing, and I told him I'd stolen a lot of his ideas.

After a while, the party dwindled down a little bit, and Bill went back out on stage and played for another fifteen minutes because he loved the piano—a Steinway grand—so much. When you give an artist the right equipment, you're going to get more than your money's worth. And that's the thing some promoters don't get—some view such provisions as cutting into their bottom line. Those Ames, Iowa concerts for public television? They would have been so superior if whoever was in charge of this important detail had provided the proper piano, and that's why Bill was upset. This is a point that can't be overstated.

While in Paris, we spent a lot of time hanging out with Francis Paudras, a commercial artist, author and patron of jazz musicians. His relationship with pianist Bud Powell was the inspiration for the movie *Round Midnight* with saxophonist Dexter Gordon in a leading acting role.[2] Musicians traveling through Paris would often gather at Francis' apartment to hang out. I still have a photo of Bill giving pianist Walter Davis a piano lesson at Francis' place. Francis followed us all around Paris with a video camera and made a film about it, but I've never seen it. I'd like to track that down as there's footage of me talking with Klook backstage after the show.

Spread out over nearly a month, the band played a dozen venues across the continent, traveling by train and plane. When it was over, we headed back to Paris for our return flight to the states. We got to a hotel at Charles de Gaulle Airport in the wee hours, completely frazzled and tired but feeling good about going home. We had an early departure for John F. Kennedy International Airport in New York, so we rented rooms at the airport and headed to a restaurant when it opened at 6:00 a.m. We were the first ones in there, and as none of us spoke French, Bill took it upon himself to order. "We'd like eggs," he said, adding, "You know, eggs?" And then he clucked like a chicken and flapped his arms like wings, which the waitress understood and smiled at. "And we want bacon," he said, snorting like a pig. The waitress now looked at him like he was out of his freaking mind, at which point Marc turned to me and said, "Let's see how he handles home fried potatoes."

***

Bill and Stan Getz had known each other and worked together for many years, and I think I can best characterize Bill's relationship with Stan as guarded. Obviously they had a common bond in the music but, beyond that, I know that Bill did not consider Stan a close personal friend. We departed as a group for Lyon, France with the exception of Stan who had flown out the day before to see his doctor. Upon arrival at baggage claim, the entire group was set upon by the airport police and taken away for a very thorough search. According to the police, they had received an "anonymous phone tip" that some of the musicians were carrying drugs. As luck would have it, Bill, who was sitting in first class, got off the plane first and looking very civilian in his winter coat and glasses coasted right through baggage to the other side of security. From there, full of righteous indignation, he accused the police of unfair harassment and brutality. I finally walked over to him and suggested that he go to the hotel before they decided to search him. In all my years on the road, I have never been so thoroughly searched as this particular time. The police literally took my drums apart even looking in the hollow chambers of my cymbal stands and other hardware. Of course, they found nothing. I am not implying that I was a saint during this period, but I was smart enough to know that an international drug bust was something to avoid.

What happened next was worthy of a Keystone Kops episode. The police finally found a tiny roach (slang for a butt of marijuana) among the possessions of Stan's drummer, and they promptly and with great fanfare took him into a detention room for questioning. They sat him at a table and placed the roach in front of him demanding an explanation. At one point during the interrogation all the police officers got up to confer out of the suspects' earshot, which also took them out of his sight. Now besides being a swinging player, this drummer was also very street savvy, so he grabbed the roach and quickly swallowed it. When the cops returned, he asked for some water which they supplied and he washed it down! When they realized that the evidence was gone, they had to release him and we all made our way to the venue and made the gig.

Later that night Bill called me to come to his room. He was in a very agitated state, claiming that he saw someone peering in through his window. This would have been virtually impossible in a high-rise hotel with Bill's room near the top with no balcony. He went on to say that he was so paranoid, he flushed about $500 worth of cocaine down the toilet! At this point I just wanted the tour to finish, so I could go home.

Chapter 14

Hanging with Bill 4

When I joined up with Bill, the trio wore uniforms: heavy, dark velour sport coats. I tried on Eliot Zigmund's, which was 10 times bigger than me. I just about died. It was like wearing curtains from a men's club—no way was I going to wear that. Bill and Marc agreed it was time to retire them.

This led to a band trip to SYMS,[1] a discount men's clothing chain in New Jersey. Once there, we went our own way to find what we each liked. When we reconnected to compare sartorial taste, it turned out we were miles from each other. By this time, Bill's fashion sense, by his own admission, was strictly off the rack and a matter of convenience. In fact, when Bill won the Grammy for *Conversations with Myself* in 1964, the sport coat and trousers he wore to the ceremony belonged to Woody Herman! Gene Lees, the late jazz journalist, told this story in his book of anecdotes, *Meet Me At Jim and Andy's: Jazz Musicians and Their World.*[2] Turns out that Gene, a good friend of Woody's and Bill's, was looking after Woody's apartment. Meanwhile, Bill had nothing decent to wear for the ceremony. So Gene loaned him Woody's blue blazer and gray slacks. A few days later, Bill, wearing the same blazer, showed up to lunch with Woody and Gene.

Woody recognized the blazer, marked with the monogram over the breast pocket. And Bill looked at Woody and said, "How do you like the monogram, WH? It stands for William Heavens." Woody broke up in laughter.

Eventually, we found an outfit we could live with: sport coats, matching slacks and open white-collared shirts. (François Lacharme graciously described these coats as "unremarkable" in his essay, *Sorrow in Soho.* See Appendix.) But while backstage in Italy in 1979, we gave up on that and agreed to wear jackets for concert stages and tours. In clubs, we'd dress a bit more casually.

In 1976, Bill summarized his feelings on fashion style with Sondra Gair on her radio show *Jazz Artist Interview* on WBEZ Chicago. Gair asked about his rather straight-laced appearance on many album covers, and his reply revealed just a bit of mischief.

"I made a point of it, almost," he said. "I used to kind of just resent the copy mentality, (meaning) that if Dizzy (Gillespie) wore a beret and tortoise shell rimmed glasses, there'd be three thousand others out there like that. And so it always used to make me feel good to walk in looking like the worst square that happened, and then be able to go up and play .... And I don't know, I sort of maybe, somewhat, had that kind of thing going anyhow, sort of more of a straight approach, too, because I didn't think about style or appearance as far as clothes or my presentation of *self* or anything like that. I just wasn't concerned with it, so I just naturally more or less selected the *(everyday look)*, which would be going to any barber shop to get a haircut and get the clothes off the rack that everybody else is getting."[3]

Chapter 15

The Village Vanguard:
Turn Out the Stars
May 27 to June 8, 1980

More than once, I heard Max Gordon call the Village Vanguard, the club he opened in 1935, an "elegant dump." Indeed, the décor would never merit a story in *Architectural Digest*. He was even known to have said, *Don't make it too nice or else customers will stay too long!* But Gordon's vigilant emphasis on a club that respected and encouraged jazz transformed the subterranean room into one of the world's most celebrated venues. His successors, led by his late wife Lorraine and now their daughter, Deborah, and other loyal employees, continued that tradition. And the results are indisputable. Virtually every major jazz artist has performed at the Vanguard. More than 190 album titles include the words "Live at the Village Vanguard," including landmark recordings by Sonny Rollins, John Coltrane, and Bill Evans.[1] For our trio, the Vanguard was like home base, a place to experiment and grow our sound. So I was thrilled when Bill decided our next album would be a trio date recorded live at the storied club. There is a certain chemistry to the place that just made playing there a joy, and to be a part of a live recording at the Village Vanguard was very special.

Gordon, a Lithuanian immigrant of boundless enthusiasm, was a permanent fixture at the Greenwich Village haunt (Lorraine often called it his living room).[2] He would stay every night until closing time (most gigs lasted three sets, winding up at about 1:30 a.m.). But one Tuesday during a trio date, apparently deciding he wasn't needed, Max left early. Seeing a fairly empty room, Bill skipped the obligatory third set and headed home early to his apartment across the Hudson River in Fort Lee, New Jersey. One customer complained to Bill, who offered to refund his money. Quitting early was also fine by me. By then, I'd moved to Lake Katrine, a two-hour drive, at least. Anyway, when Max found out the next day, he was really mad and had some words with Bill. He also stayed every night until closing for the rest of the week's engagement.

Likening the room to a dump was a bit extreme, and in fact so many clubs at the time in New York City appeared similar in the daytime. Nonetheless, that didn't dissuade fans, who flocked there for its excellent acoustics. But I should say that in recent years, the club has been nicely upgraded. Even the men's room! I was packing up my drums a few years ago when a plumber arrived to do the remodel and referred to the original fixtures as "collectible!"

Patrons still enter off 7th Avenue under a long canopy, descending to a triangular-like basement some twenty feet down a stairway. During one of our engagements, Max got mugged and knocked down the stairs in the afternoon when opening up but showed up for work that night, Band-Aids and all—a testament to his unflagging energy. At the bottom of the stairwell, you are greeted at another door and shown into the club. To your immediate right is the bar, which extends all the way to the back wall. Besides close-quarter table seats, you can also sit at the bar. Turn left from the entrance into a hallway and you head for the kitchen (which doubles as the office and where most musicians hang out on breaks) and the men's room (follow the red line on the floor). Back there, another flight of stairs ascends to the alley behind the club.

Numerous photos of jazz legends line the walls, including one of Bill's famous trio with bassist Scott LaFaro and drummer Paul Motian—the band that recorded his 1961 masterpiece, *Sunday at the Village Vanguard*. It was one of several shot at a small table during intermission that week. Bill stares down from yet another photo (sans glasses) while not too far away you see Miles Davis looking so bored, he practically says, "So what?"

Back inside the main room, a split-level follows the far wall on the right and continues to the stage. A padded bench lines the wall with small tables for customers; the only drawback is a large support beam that blocks the view for a couple of tables. As you look at the stage from the front, the piano is on the left, which leaves room for the bass and drums on the right. Bill told me that in earlier years, customers sat on what is now the stage, and the piano resided on the main level.

When Bill first arrived in New York, he'd play solo piano there during intermissions. One night as he played, the maître d' walked a couple between Bill and the keyboard to reach a table behind him! Intermissions offered audiences an opportunity to chat and relax, so the noise level rose with conversation, thus making the job of playing purely functional. On one noisy night, Bill looked up to see Miles leaning on the piano, enjoying the music. Word was spreading about this young, bespectacled pianist.

We worked six to eight weeks a year at the Vanguard and always looked forward to it because it meant two weeks at home, as much as four times a year and an opportunity to play for all our friends. The room was packed every night, especially Friday and Saturday, with fans and a who's who of jazz luminaries. Everyone stopped in to hear the trio, especially when the word got out that things were starting to click musically with Bill, Marc and me. Tony Bennett, Dexter Gordon, Woody Shaw, John Abercrombie, John Scofield and Pat Metheny (and his entire band) would often show up. Musicians would sit in occasionally, including John Clayton on bass in 1979 before he moved to Holland, and tenor saxophonist Joe Lovano, recently off Woody Herman's band. Both were up to the task. What I learned from these experiences was that Bill stayed open to players of all styles and enjoyed stepping away from the trio format once in a while. Also, with a horn we got to enjoy Bill's amazing *comping* (jazz lingo for "accompaniment"). As a soloist, you had better be saying something special because Bill's melodic comping could draw the listener away. Our shows were not without a few laughs. Most performers would bristle if a large number of fans left in the middle of a set. But this happened occasionally, particularly on Fridays and Saturdays, when busloads of international tourists left *en masse* to visit the next point of interest.

From my vantage point, watching and listening to Bill at the Vanguard was an incredible experience. He was so focused on the music that he would completely draw you in. Nothing seemed to interfere with his power of concentration. On "Nardis," for example, Bill often played four or five unaccompanied choruses to start the tune, during which time his glasses would slowly descend down the bridge of his nose until I was certain they would land on the keyboard. But every time at the last second, his hand flew up and pushed them back in place without the slightest interference to his playing. I could almost see and hear his brain at work, as he would simultaneously weave ideas from Marc and me into his own solos and comping. I don't remember who said, "There are no wrong notes in jazz," but Bill proved this true night after night with us.

Because of the Village Vanguard's ideal atmosphere, the trio developed quickly. I've listened to hours of recordings I made of us (from a cassette player under the piano), and the growth was obvious from night to night. Bill was always clear about everything on the bandstand; all you had to do was listen and react. Established repertoire was easy for longtime fans like Marc and me because those arrangements had largely stayed the same since the trio's inception. Bill had a format he used when adding a tune to the book: pick the tune, pick the key, the tempo, make any alterations to the original harmony and make the arrangement. His view was that once you have a set arrangement, the only thing you really have to focus on is the improvisation, which is the most important thing. There is a recording available of Bill and bassist Scott LaFaro using this approach to prepare "My Foolish Heart" for the *Waltz for Debby* album just days before the gig. In this session, you can hear just how much Scott LaFaro's suggestions helped to create this arrangement.

We experienced the same thing with new tunes we added to the book and also in reworking older material. For example, Marc and I deliberately suspended the time during the last eight bars of Tadd Dameron's "If You Could See Me Now." The tempo was constant but not stated, giving Bill's melody a unique, floating feeling. On Joe Zawinul's "Midnight Mood," I'd switch to brushes for Marc's solo and the last melody until the coda, where I went back to sticks to give the finale a dynamic rise. Small things to be sure, but I could track Bill hearing it and responding. We were making this book ours.

Once the Vanguard recording dates were set—June 4, 5, 6 and 8, 1980—a different piano had to be brought in because the house keyboard had too many miles on it. I felt a little embarrassed about the number of microphones on the drums. There were so many; everything but the stool had a mic on it! I looked over at the piano, and there were two visible mics while the drum set had 10! But I must admit that the recording quality was excellent throughout thanks to engineer Malcolm Addey and his assistant Jon Bobenko.

Originally Helen Keane had decided on three nights of recording—enough material for one vinyl LP (remember those, folks?). Bill wanted to record every night because you just never know when "it" is going to happen. As it turned out, we didn't record on Friday night of the run, and that turned out to be Bill's favorite night of the week. But what we got was still very good. It's understandable that when the recorders were off, we all relaxed a little more and just played.

For reasons unknown, these masters lay dormant for more than 15 years after Bill died. I had cassette copies as did Marc and Helen, and eventually we just gave up on the idea of them ever being released. After Helen's death in 1996, Warner Brothers issued the entire week's output that year in a six-CD box set, called *Turn Out the Stars: The Final Village Vanguard Recordings* (the title is taken from one of Bill's better known compositions).

Ultimately, they released some multiple recordings of the same tunes (hence, various takes of "Nardis," "My Romance," etc.), which Bill likely would have opposed. But in retrospect, it's historical in nature. The idea is you play the same tunes every night four nights in a row to get your best tracks. You have a different audience every night, so no one's suffering here. But when you see the number of recordings that some artists have released that include the same repertoire, you understand why Bill wouldn't go that route. It's just too much of the same thing and only serves the jazz fanatic that wants to compare one outtake to another.

For that gig, Bill included several new tunes he wrote during this period: "Your Story," Letter to Evan" (for his son), "Tiffany" (for my daughter), "Knit For Mary F" (for a longtime fan of Bill's who knitted sweaters as gifts for him; this was his way of returning the favor), and "Yet Ne'er Broken." The last was an anagram for someone Bill knew, and was originally titled "Out Of The Blue" because Bill said the tune just shot out of the sky and into his brain and then on to the piano. As I said earlier, the box set features numerous takes of the same titles because we were tracking for one LP and looking for the best performances of each tune. Normally during a weeklong engagement, Bill would vary the program much more. Ultimately the final product got great reviews. Allmusic.com gave it four stars with critic Scott Yanow noting the band's interplay bordered on "telepathic ... The playing throughout these consistently inventive performances ranks up there with the Evans-Scott LaFaro-Paul Motian trio of 20 years earlier."[3]

Bill had said in print and to several friends that the trio with Marc and me was similar in spirit to the trio with Scott and Paul. Speaking in 1980 to Michael Bloom in *Klacto*, a Hawaiian jazz newsletter, Bill said, "it's a hell of a trio. It's at least as good as the first trio if not the best I've ever had."[4]

I am equally surprised and embarrassed by this comment, but this transcript quote from Bill during an interview in 1979 may shed more light on why he loved this trio so much. In the interview on WBEZ in Chicago, radio host Dick Buckley asked Bill how he dealt with out-of-tune pianos.

"The chemistry of this trio is very good," Bill told Buckley. "When something is negative, this trio is such that it works you out of it. And whereas if the chemistry wasn't good, I might have gone downhill. Instead I kept going uphill and by the third set, I was really enjoying myself, despite the fact that the piano was out of tune."[5]

Bill's comment to Buckley shows that it was the chemistry of the three musicians that drove this renewed creativity in Bill, not necessarily the individual talents. I think all of Bill's trios were great because they had a great piano player!

Joe—

HAPPY BIRTHDAY!! The first 32 are the hardest ——

I have a present for you — it is the decision to write a feature for you called "Joe's Time" — But I did not want to rush it so for now accept, please, the intent which I will do as soon as the idea takes shape.

My Dr. wants to talk to you. If you don't get a call from him by 2 will give you his number and via his message since you can remind him — or I will...

Anyhow — as I said you will be making a rapid but careful and safe drive to Woodstock for the supreme birthday present. — Evans is infallible!

always —
Bill

P.S. Press play button on cassette

Bill wrote me this letter on my 32nd birthday of his plans to write a feature tune for me. I was staying in Bill's apartment that week. This letter was waiting for me when I got back from my gig at Michael's Pub in New York City. I was blown away by Bill's version of "Happy Birthday" on his cassette player that was sitting next to the letter. I have listened to this recording on my birthday every year since 1980. *Courtesy of Joe La Barbera.*

While I'm proud of all the material on these recordings, none warm my heart more than "Tiffany," Bill's homage to my daughter. Earlier that year in February, I was crashing at Bill's while doing a weeklong engagement in Manhattan (Bill always let me stay to avoid the two-hour drive to my home in upstate New York). It was during the week of my birthday, February 22. That night, I returned from the gig to Bill's Fort Lee apartment to find a letter for me and a note on a cassette player that said, "press play." So first I read the letter in which he offered his congratulations and some classic Evans advice about life and so on. He also went on to say that he wanted to write a tune featuring me for the trio, called "Joe's Time," but he didn't want to rush it. He wanted to think about it, and he wanted me to accept the intent. Then I hit the play button on the cassette to hear Bill play four choruses of "Happy Birthday" in his inimitable style. At the end, he said, "Happy birthday, kid. I'd give you my lecture on the evils of drugs, but it's late and you just have to look at me as an example." So he was going through a reflective moment there. I have listened to this recording on my birthday every year since then.

A few nights later, when I got back to Bill's, he was waiting up for me to say that my wife had called and I was to get home fast. I called my friend Ron Davis to cover the final nights at Michael's Pub for me (where I'd been playing with Carol Sloane, Jimmy Rowles and George Mraz) and drove home. Tiffany was born a few days later on February 29 (a Leap Year baby!). So I called Bill with the news, and a couple of days later, he called our house and played a tune he'd written for Tiffany over the phone. Of course, my wife and I were both very moved by this, and I gratefully accepted that song in lieu of any feature that might have been forthcoming for me in the trio. I thought that tune for Tiffany was fantastic. It was all the more amazing because it really captures her personality, the woman she has grown up to be. It's a lovely waltz, upbeat, with a positive feeling. And there was no way for Bill to know that. A few weeks after Tiffany was born, Bill and Marc drove all the way up from Manhattan one night. We ordered in some food and he met Tiffany; she was probably two months old at that point. Maybe even less. In swaddling clothes.

My daughter, Tiffany La Barbera-Palmer, who Bill wrote a song for when she was born. At 16, Tiffany would write lyrics to this tune (unbeknown to me at the time), which would eventually become the published version. I point with pride to her name on the same piece of music with Bill Evans. *Photo by Tiffany La Barbera-Palmer. Courtesy of Tiffany La Barbera-Palmer.*

When Bill and I later spoke about this, and I told him how grateful we both were for him writing that tune, he said he got a lot of requests from people asking, "Can you write a tune for my wife?" or "Can you write a tune for my daughter?" Or this and that and the other thing. And he would always say to them, "This is not an on-demand process. This is something

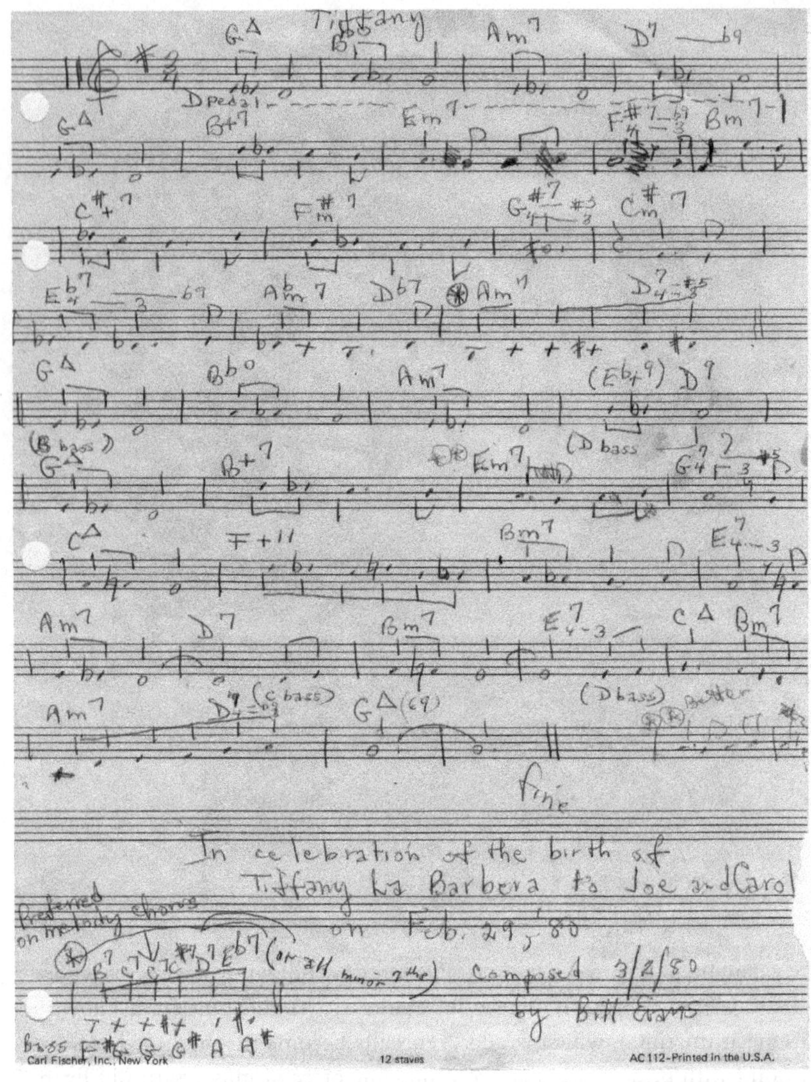

The "Tiffany" lead sheet in Bill Evans' hand, including instructions for alternate harmony at the end of the bridge and a dedication at the bottom of the page. *Courtesy of Joe La Barbera.*

that has to come from the heart." You know he obviously felt something to want to do that.

Meanwhile, Bill promised that Tiffany would get 50 percent of the composer's credit, which meant 50 percent of any royalties generated by performances, sales, or airplay of the song. This was incredibly generous. But the offer was never formalized. After Bill passed away, Helen had no way to verify the agreement, so Tiffany was not eligible for royalties.

As luck would have it, in 1997, vocalist Tierney Sutton was preparing to record the song, but there were no published lyrics. At that time, Tiffany was studying vocals with Tierney and mentioned that she had written lyrics to it when she was 16 years old (big surprise to Dad!). Tierney checked them out and loved them, so when I learned of this, I contacted Judy Bell at The Richmond Organization, Bill's publisher. Judy accepted the lyrics. Now Tiffany's name is on the song and, mind you, it's not about the money. It just means so much to me to see her name right next to Bill Evans. (The song appears on Sutton's 2001 album, *Blue in Green*, in a medley with Bill's classic, "Waltz for Debby.")

Tiffany La Barbera-Palmer recalled this episode …

Tierney's album, *Blue in Green*, had to be the catalyst to write the lyrics because I didn't start writing music until I was in my 20s, and I think I was 17 at the time. Up until then, I wrote a lot of prose, but I wasn't writing music.

At that time, I was living during the school year with my mom and stepfather in Phoenix. My bedroom door faced their door, and I wrote and taped the lyrics to the door. I couldn't bring myself to hand them to anyone. You have to admit it's pretty narcissistic to write lyrics to your own song [laughs].

As I get older, it's hard to hear the song in public without crying. Because of that song, I got into ASCAP (American Society of Composers, Authors and Publishers, the agency which monitors songs for performance royalties), and in many ways began doing the things I'm most proud of. I recorded an original album of original, progressive rock music with my cousins, and I've done a lot of musical theater. The last show I appeared in, the company used a photo of me in the lead that was used as a promo photo in BroadwayWorld.com.

Dad's right. I don't know how Bill knew, but he wrote a song that is absolutely my personality. Sometimes I worry that I didn't live up to it. It's upbeat and a little sad. Today, it's something both dad and I have in common. We both have original copies of the sheet music in our homes.

My first real romantic relationship was with a piano player named Randy Ingram, who played for Tierney's vocal classes. It started while I was attending Santa Monica City College. I met him at one of dad's gigs. Around the time of my birthday, he was playing in a little club on the top floor of the Dorothy Chandler Pavilion. Randy had two nights there, and he played "Tiffany" on the first night. That began the relationship [big laugh]. He always played this when we were dating, and we were together for a while after that.

When Eric, my husband, and I got engaged, dad had a gig upstairs at Vitello's in Studio City with his quintet, and he had them play it. In 2014, four years after we married, dad played at the Village Vanguard with pianist Enrico Pieranunzi and Marc Johnson. Dad; his wife, Gillian; Eric; and I all have February birthdays, so we celebrated them at the club, and dad got it put on the set list—and it was beautiful.

I teach at a private school with a wonderful man, Dr. Robert Farrar. He teaches history at Polytechnic and African-American History at Pasadena City College. And he's a big jazz fan. Whenever he sees me, and there's an opportunity to sit down and talk, he says, "I just need a little background music." And he plays "Tiffany" on Spotify.[6]

Chapter 16

Hanging with Bill 5

In a Hotel Lobby

On one of our European tours, we performed in Holland and stayed at a nice old hotel in the city center. Marc and I were already seated in the lobby when Bill arrived in a very playful mood and sat down at a well-worn piano nearby. When he started to play, it was not what you would expect from this jazz giant but rather more like an elementary school student struggling with a lesson. I'm sure that many of us have experienced this same scenario while sitting in a hotel lobby somewhere as a patron tries his or her hand at the piano.

Most passersby paid Bill no mind until an elegantly dressed older couple entered the lobby and paused at the doorway. The woman noticed Bill's attempts and walked over to the piano and moved him aside to sit next to him on the bench. She then proceeded to play only marginally better than Bill's put-on, while Bill sat beside her "oohing" and "aahing" to her delight. When she finished, he complimented her and never let on his true talent, allowing her a moment of glory.

***

Montreal Airport, February 26, 1979

After a week-long engagement at the Rising Sun Celebrity Jazz Club in Montreal, we flew back to New York. While waiting at the airport for departure, I noticed an airport police officer staring intently at Bill who looked very bad at the time. The cop gradually worked his way closer, and my radar went off. Bill's physical appearance—jaundice-like complexion, exhausted, head perennially down—would have raised suspicions to any trained D.E.A. official, so I approached as well, hoping to intercede somehow. When the officer was in front of Bill, he asked his name and when Bill responded, the officer said, "I thought it was you! Man, you sounded so great last night. I caught both sets." My heart eventually slowed to a normal rate somewhere over Manhattan.

***

No Good Deed Goes Unpunished

For one of our overseas trips, I decided to help Bill out and save him some money for cab fare. So on my way to JFK International Airport, I stopped to pick him up at his apartment in Fort Lee, New Jersey. We agreed on a suitable time so I could drop Bill and my drums off at the terminal and then go to the long term parking lot with enough time to make our flight.

When I arrived at Bill's place, he wasn't even packed. It took him a long time to get it together, so by the time we left, we were right smack in the middle of Manhattan rush hour. By the time we got to JFK, I was forced to park in the short-term lot—for two weeks! Back in 1979, this cost over $200. Bill gave me around $75 when we returned from the trip.

***

Sam Distefano

During the Korean War, Bill Evans was stationed near Chicago at Fort Sheridan where he had enlisted in 1951. He made a lot of friends during his time in Chicago, many of whom would remain in contact throughout his lifetime. Sam Distefano was one such friend, and their meeting is an interesting story that Sam told me over dinner in Las Vegas while I worked there with Tony Bennett. Sam was the entertainment director at the Riviera Hotel, where he'd booked Tony.

When Sam received his draft notice, he sought out the Fort Sheridan band in the hopes of auditioning and being accepted into it. Chicago was his hometown so it made perfect sense. He caught a concert of the 5th Army Band somewhere in Chicago, and it was here that he first met Bill. Being an Army band, they played all the usual military marches and light classics, but at some point, a grand piano was wheeled out, followed by a bespectacled young man who proceeded to play some of the best jazz piano Sam had ever heard.

After the concert Sam introduced himself, and they spoke for a while. Bill asked Sam what was happening in his life, and Sam told him about the draft notice and his desire to audition. Bill immediately took Sam in to see the commanding officer. "This is my good friend Sam Distefano," Bill told the C.O. "He's a great musician, and we could really use him in the band." The C.O. was most receptive to anyone Bill recommended and said fine. However, when he asked Sam what instrument he played, Sam's reply was piano. The C.O. explained that the unit only had one slot for that M.O.S. (Military Occupational Specialty)—and Bill was it. What they really needed were piccolo players. Hearing this, Bill chimed in, "He's a great piccolo player, too!"

Well, that sealed the deal. Sam was told to report for an audition in the following weeks. Meanwhile, Sam was in shock and told Bill he couldn't play the piccolo at all, and *Where did he get that idea anyway?* Bill told Sam not to worry, that he would teach him enough to get him into the band … which he did. You see, besides playing the piano, Bill played first chair flute in the orchestra at Southeastern Louisiana University.

***

In spite of success and worldwide acclaim, Bill was still prone to self-doubt. It's hard to imagine that someone as artistically great as Bill would suffer the same misgivings that a lot of us mere mortals experience about our playing. Bill used to ask me to tape our gigs on my Uher cassette recorder, which I did night after night, and he'd take them home and listen. Later he would give them back and usually say, "Oh man, I sound awful. Erase that one please!" Every once in a while, he would hear something that he felt was worthy, and I don't mind telling you that I was elated to be even a small part of what he liked.

One night at the Vanguard while we were playing "But Not For Me," Bill quoted "Jumpin' With Symphony Sid" at the top of the second half of the tune and I fell out, incredibly amused over that idea. Bill never quoted tunes during his solos, always placing a much higher demand on his creative resources, and this quote in particular is just a riff. When I commented on it later, I told him that I liked it and that it fit perfectly, but Bill felt differently. "Man, when you start quoting tunes like that in your solo, it's time to take it out," Bill said. "In fact, from now on I'm going to use that as a cue to end my solos!" He actually did that a few times, but the novelty of it eventually wore off. More than likely, the urgency of his remaining time would not allow him to waste any of it, especially when it came to playing. Jazz was, after all, serious business for Bill.

Chapter 17

Last Days: Europe, 1980
July 14 to August 15

By July 1980, Europe beckoned again, this time for a month-long tour, including two weeks at Ronnie Scott's Jazz Club, London's premiere late-night hang. I was still in denial about Bill's health, but in hindsight there was plenty of evidence to show he was spiraling downward. When I look at photographs today, it's startling to see the difference between his appearance then—a walking skeleton, shedding pounds, barely eating—and when I joined the band—comparatively speaking, a picture of health.

Perhaps just as telling was an episode at JFK International Airport as we waited to board our plane. This is the one time Bill's drug addiction got the better of him. Bill and Helen told us in advance that we'd be paid $450 per concert for the tour. I had already calculated what I could realistically expect to earn and was finally able to deliver some good financial news at home. The euphoria was cut short at the departure lounge. Bill told us that due to his own financial needs, he was cutting my and Marc's salary to $250 each per concert. He said that most musicians would gladly go on a tour for this amount of money but would understand if we refused. Refusing would, of course, mean no tour at all and no money. It appeared to me that Bill had likely taken a draw on the pay and spent it, which meant the trio was taking a back seat to Bill's addiction. If he had said that he was in a jam, perhaps owed child support, taxes, whatever, this would have gone down a lot better. But he just laid it out—take it or leave it—and this is what upset me the most.

I think Bill was possibly hoping I would say no to the offer, so that he and Marc could do the tour as a duo or pick up a European drummer, thus saving more money. More than being upset, I was really hurt by Bill's actions. The feeling among the three of us had grown way beyond employment to something of a family nature. To me, Bill was like a brother, and I'm sure he viewed Marc as a son. In any event, I took the tour simply because there was no alternative. My personal life was already under a strain. The amount of money I was able to earn as a jazz drummer fell short of the lifestyle expected at home. I totally get it now, but at the time, I was counting on the money to support my family. What was I supposed to do? Walk away? I couldn't say no.

Bill had never behaved like this—quite the contrary. Until now he always took care of Marc and me as a matter of pride and mutual respect. He once said of me in an interview that I "was dedicated to playing quality music and ... willing to make the concessions of travel and the concessions of dues toward that end."[1] He understood what it meant to be separated from his family as well as being the primary breadwinner. Even though he was estranged from his wife Nenette, he still provided for her and young Evan, their son. My situation was similar with a wife and newborn daughter, Tiffany, depending on me. Obviously, Bill had reached a critical turning point where his physical dependency took precedence over all else.

We opened in Barcelona on July 14, then hopscotched to Milan for a concert four days later. Then we flew to London for the dates at Ronnie Scott's.

Along with the Village Vanguard, musicians and fans alike regard Ronnie Scott's as one of the most important jazz clubs in the world. Saxophonist Ronnie Scott opened the venue almost 60 years ago in a London West End basement so musicians had a place to jam. In 1965, Scott relocated the club to its current home in the city's Soho district. Every major jazz artist has performed there, from Sarah Vaughn to Count Basie to Elvin Jones to

Stan Getz.[2] The club has also hosted a big band led by Rolling Stones drummer Charlie Watts and singer-songwriters like Tom Waits and Mark Knopfler.[3] Prior to the engagement with Bill, I worked there once with Chuck Mangione in 1974 opposite Stephane Grappelli.

As usual for club gigs—and just like the Village Vanguard—we played for two weeks (almost unheard of today!), so naturally we looked forward to settling in for a while in one place. Bill had lots of fans in London, including celebrities such as actors Peter Sellers, Marty Feldman and John Le Mesurier, and numerous local musicians. Drummer Kenny Clare was a friend of mine from the Woody Herman days, and I spent an enjoyable afternoon at his home with his family while in town. The club was full every night and the music—captured on disc—was quite good overall.

Ronnie Scott was a debonair and congenial host with a razor sharp wit, who emceed most nights and besides being a wonderful tenor player was also a very funny fellow. His well-worn jokes were legendary to anyone who regularly frequented the club and no matter how many times you heard the gag, it was still entertaining because of his deadpan delivery. For example: "Ladies and gentlemen, I have just received word that our men's room attendant has given notice this evening. It seems he can no longer tolerate the smell coming from the kitchen!" Or casting his gaze over an unresponsive crowd: "This is the first time I have ever seen an oil painting smoke!"

Pete King, Ronnie's right-hand man, managed the club on a daily basis. A bit larger than the Vanguard, Ronnie Scott's sits at street level. But the vibe is similar because the music is the main attraction and a strict listening policy is enforced. Typically, with Bill's concerts, the audience respected the music and came to listen.

Laurie joined us on this trip for the two weeks in London and looked after Bill all day in the hotel, getting him ready for the gig at night. I can't remember the name of the hotel we stayed at, but I remember it was a distance from the club. So we had to be picked up and dropped off each night. Marc and I passed the time exploring London's Soho neighborhood during the day. One afternoon we each got a call from Bill asking us to come to his room right away. We arrived together, assuming it was time to get paid. This close to the end, it was possible that Bill was paid, and most bandleaders would not want the responsibility of holding on to that much cash. Or maybe just a change in the itinerary. The room smelled of smoke and charred "something." Bill was on the bed, looking a bit sheepish. He told us we needed to help him turn over the king-size mattress on his bed. We pulled back the sheets to reveal a very large hole burned through the cover, stuffing and springs. He had fallen asleep in bed with a lit cigarette but fortunately awoke before the fire became a blaze. We opened the windows to let the smoke and odor out, and turned the mattress over to conceal the damage. It was probably weeks before that hole was discovered, if ever. This episode immediately brought to mind an article in *DownBeat* I read years earlier of the death of trumpeter Joe Gordon who had a similar experience but never woke up again.

During the run there, a close friend of Bill's asked to record the gig. I don't recall the man's name, but he clearly had Bill's permission to make an audio recording of the gig. It wasn't a surreptitious act, like someone had a microphone sticking out of a purse. He set up a reel-to-reel recorder on the table right in front of the piano. (I think he may have set up three mics, because he captured everything—drums, piano and bass—in decent quality.) Unfortunately, the piano is out of tune.

I suspect Bill worked out a deal with the person, although I don't know what it would have been. But this wasn't an isolated incident, and people who asked Bill if they could record a gig used the same line: *It's just for my personal use. It'll never see the light of day.* Bill may have realized at some point that such promises were made to be broken or maybe he didn't care. And I get why companies are eager to release these recordings. They all say the same thing: *We owe it to the fans.* People want to hear it. Fine.

Several other shows from this tour wound up as legitimate videos. A concert at Molde, Norway was filmed in its entirety. Segments of our performance at the Gouvy Jazz Festival in Belgium are featured in a documentary by the French trumpeter, filmmaker and photographer Léon Terjanian. (Both are easily found on YouTube.) Several concerts, including shows in Rome and Barcelona, were also recorded and later shown on European television. (See Appendix for list of recordings and videos.)

As I mentioned earlier, there were three occasions on which I had to physically hold Bill as he weathered an emotional crisis. The second occurred during a stop in Copenhagen at the Jazzhus Montmartre (better known in the states as the Club Montmartre). By this time, Bill's substance abuse was consuming him, and he was in constant need, both physically and emotionally.

We did our sound check and took a dinner break, at which time Bill went upstairs to rest in an apartment that the club kept for visiting artists. After a while Bill sent for me. He asked me to go downstairs to the club and pick up a package from some guy who was waiting. I was reticent and Bill sensed that, but he knew he could count on me. I did as he asked and then stalled for quite a while. I was still naive enough to believe that Bill could be brought back to good physical health, so I was not inclined to bring him the drugs. Marc and I talked about it, and we both agreed that things had gotten pretty bad as far as Bill's health was concerned. Marc sympathized with my dilemma, but the decision to give Bill what he needed was up to me alone. My motives for doing what was asked at the time are unclear at this point. Possibly I felt a sense of obligation or maybe it was completely self-serving: get what Bill needs and let's play the gig. Bill only asked me a couple of times for help in this regard in any event.

In the end, I relented and went upstairs to the apartment. When I opened the door, I found Bill standing in the center of the room shaking violently from head to toe. I grabbed a blanket off the bed, wrapped him in it and then threw us both on the bed until the heat from the blanket as well as my body heat warmed him. As we lay there, he looked at me and said, "Man, for a minute there I thought you weren't coming back, but then I knew you could never be that cruel." With this sentence Bill eliminated any resolve I had in getting him to stop, and he showed me the severity of the consequences if he didn't get what he needed.

Bill spent the rest of the night in bed recovering while Marc and I went on stage with Jørgen Emborg on piano and Bob Rockwell, an American tenor player in Copenhagen at the time.

At a concert in Reggio Calabria on Italy's southern coast, Bill experienced a cognitive breakdown. It was the one time in all the gigs we played where his brain didn't connect with his hands. I don't exactly recall which tune we were playing, but it was something from our standard repertoire—a tune he knew very well and he lost it. He completely lost the form and played in the wrong key. He came to me after the gig with surprise in his eyes. He flatly stated that this had never happened before, and he was shaken by it. This was as shocking to me as it was to Bill because I'd never heard him play one wrong note.

By the end of the tour, things deteriorated even more. Originally, we were scheduled to finish with five dates in Italy. Bill should have taken a few days off for his health before the flight home. But tour manager Wim Wigt squeezed a show in at the last minute. It was a private party on August 15 (the eve of Bill's 51st birthday) at the home of Fritz Feltens in Bad Hönningen, Germany. Looking back now, the booking may have been a desperation move because Bill had likely been drawing money ahead on the tour. Feltens, an architect and ardent Evans fan, had made elaborate preparations for the event and gave Bill an expensive watch as a thank you gift.

Unfortunately, upon arrival after an hour-long drive, Bill realized he'd left something at the hotel and insisted on returning to retrieve it. This delayed proceedings even further, but eventually we did play. (Helen Keane negotiated the agreement, which allowed Feltens to record the show for his own personal use. Famous last words! The West Wind label released it on LP in 1989 as *His Last Concert in Germany*.)

After the concert, it was time to get paid for the tour. Even though our salaries had already been nearly halved, Bill didn't have enough to pay us. I remember him saying in pleading frustration, "You guys must have drawn something." Neither Marc nor I had asked for a dime during the entire tour, which in hindsight was a mistake. Most road veterans will tell you to draw ahead on your salary, but I never felt this was necessary with Bill.

This tour was the only time in the trio's existence that things like this happened. Bill always took care of business. So Marc did me a solid favor at this point that I will never forget. He said, "You know, Bill, Joe's got a family. Pay Joe and then you can pay me when we get back to New York."

I'm pretty sure that Bill settled up with Marc back in the states. I'd hate to think otherwise.

Marc Johnson recalled that experience …

After we got home, some days went by and I called Bill to see about getting paid. He told me to come by his place in Fort Lee. So the next day I got a bus to New Jersey and made my way to his apartment building. I rang the buzzer, but there was no answer.

I walked away a bit puzzled but decided to call him from a pay phone and he answered and asked, "Was that you buzzing my apartment?" I said, "Yes, it was me." He told me to never do that again, coming over without calling first. After I was properly chastised, he said, "Well, as long as you're here, come on up."

So I got a lesson in visitation etiquette from Bill Evans.

Ha![4]

Chapter 18

Last Days: Stateside
August–September 1980

With little down time after Europe, we flew to California a week later for a short tour. It started with Bill taping a solo spot August 23, on Merv Griffin's show in Los Angeles (the spot aired a month later after Bill passed). In his introduction, Merv pointed to a pile of Bill's records behind him which belonged to another guest, the late comic Phyllis Diller, who was hoping Bill would autograph them for her.

Then under the bright studio lights, Bill briskly walked out to a white Yamaha grand piano, sporting a light blue suit and open-collared shirt, looking a bit haggard. In a hyper and jittery voice, Bill offered that while most television directors urged jazz musicians to play something upbeat for a short spot, he planned to ignore that advice. "I don't get a chance to play on shows like this too often, where I reach … where I reach this many people," he said, as Griffin, a former big band singer and avid Evans fan, interrupted halfway to say, "Play anything you want." Bill then described a new tune he'd written that revolved around "one idea … repeated over and over (which) goes to different places." For some time, the tune remained untitled, until he finally called it, "Your Story." "It seemed to be making more and more of a statement, the more that we played it …

so I would like to do this, which is a little more serious than anything for your audience."

Bill played the melody without improvising, his head typically bowed, the melody winding in gentle circles. Toward the end, bassist Ray Brown and drummer Nick Ceroli (from Griffin's house band) joined in with subtle accompaniment. Griffin couldn't restrain his enthusiasm when Bill finished. "I'd want to be in that movie, whatever it is," Griffin exulted over a cheering crowd.[1]

This should have been Bill looking good, but he just looked awful. The rigors of the recent European tour seemed to have completely exhausted whatever health he had been clinging to. He was at the end of his life. It's still tough for me to watch today. But the thing is, he played well. He always played well. Doing that was so ingrained, so second nature, that it was never an issue. He made this comment over and over in interviews, referring to the *Creative Process* and "flipping a switch," how musicians sometimes felt exhausted and uninspired but once they hit the bandstand, the music revived them. I don't think that even he realized to what extent he would test this theory because toward the end he was physically incapable of standing for very long. Truly remarkable inner strength. I think he had truly mastered that concept because when he sat down at the piano, he did flip a switch, and it was—bang!—into it.

Four days later, the trio took the stage at the Hollywood Bowl under clear skies and cool temperatures for a show billed as *The Piano Masters*. It was the inauguration of the venue's *Jazz at the Bowl* series, and sharing the bill were George Shearing and Dave Brubeck. Drummer Shelly Manne emceed. I was very excited about Shelley hearing me playing with Bill. Shelly had recorded with Bill and known him for years.

Shelly was one of my favorite and most influential drummers and it was an honor to have him emceeing. Backstage I remember running into the late Jack Six, Dave Brubeck's bass player, who also played a small role in Bill Evans' legacy. Leading up to Bill's landmark *Sunday at the Village Vanguard* recording, drummer Paul Motian recorded a rehearsal with himself, Bill and Scott LaFaro playing "My Foolish Heart" and some loose improvisations with modern classical overtones. Somehow the

A program from the Hollywood Bowl, one of the trio's final concerts and another memorable evening. Besides the trio, the concert also featured Dave Brubeck and George Shearing and was emceed by none other than Shelly Manne. *Courtesy of the Los Angeles Philharmonic Archives.*

recorder (and tape) got pawned. Jack Six bought it and kept it for years. Later on, the late Phil Bailey, a jazz DJ in Louisville, Kentucky, acquired it from Jack, who later gave it to my brother John, who was a colleague at the station. That's how it saw the light of day and acquired a sacred place in my library.

From Los Angeles, we flew up to San Francisco for a week-long run at Keystone Korner, opening Sunday, August 31. By now, Bill stayed in bed all day until about 8:30 or 9:00 p.m. We'd be at the club ready to start, and the place would be packed every night. Bill would arrive a half hour late. On the first night, pianist Denny Zeitlin was in the audience, so club owner Todd Barkan, apparently nervous about keeping a crowd waiting, asked Denny to play for 30 minutes.

Pianist Denny Zeitlin, a long-time practicing psychiatrist, recalled that night …

I only played one night. The reason being that Bill was late, and Todd asked me to play a bit. So I played for about 20 or 30 minutes. When I finished, Bill had arrived and said something very nice. "I'm actually glad I was late because it gave us all a chance to hear Denny Zeitlin play."

He was a very gracious man. It felt nice to get the compliment. I knew that Bill enjoyed my work, and he knew how much I admired his. My first LP for Columbia was for flutist Jeremy Steig, called *Flute Fever*. Shortly after its release, there was a *DownBeat* Magazine Blindfold Test with Bill featuring a track from that album. Bill said the pianist was great. So when I did my first album for Columbia, *Cathexis*, in 1964, I called him up and asked for some feedback. That was a very important moment for me. I was 25 at the time. He invited me to his apartment in Manhattan. He said, "I love your music, and I'll just tell you this: Just play *your* music. Don't let anyone tell you what to play."[2]

After a one-day extension at Keystone, we hopped a red-eye flight back to New York for another week-long run in Manhattan, opening on Tuesday, September 9. Appropriately, the gig was at Fat Tuesday's, one of New York's revered jazz clubs.

Bill was now very weak but refused to go to the hospital despite repeated pleas from all of us. I drove to the club while Bill lay on the back seat of

Pianist Denny Zeitlin filled in briefly for Bill on opening night at Keystone Korner during the trio's last gigs at the storied San Francisco club. Bill enjoyed hearing Denny as he walked into the club and acknowledged his performance to the audience. *Photo by Josephine Zeitlin. Courtesy of Denny Zeitlin.*

his car. Laurie sat up front with me but kept a constant eye on Bill. We all helped Bill to the club's entrance, but he made his own way to the bandstand. One noticeable difference for this performance was that we set up using an odd stage plot: I faced Bill's back and Marc was to his right. I think this was due to the high demand for seats, so the club had to be reconfigured slightly to fit everyone in. It was not a large venue and with a full house the sound was tight. The audience was already seated and humming with anticipation. And then he gave them what they came for: He played his ass off! What he played was remarkable by any standard but even more so considering his weakened physical condition. Years later, I received a cassette in the mail anonymously from someone who was in the audience that night. The fidelity is terrible, but what he played is amazing.

Pianist Richie Beirach attended the last night that Bill played at Fat Tuesday's. He recalled that night …

I was at Bill's final night at Fat Tuesday's in New York City in 1980. I will never forget it. It was bittersweet because Bill looked absolutely horrendous—very gaunt, much too thin for his big frame. His hair was unruly, uncut and looked matted and not his usual clean self. His shirt—Jesus, he wore that striped shirt many times without washing it.

I said hello. He knew me, of course, but he had a strange unfocused look in his eyes like somebody was after him—furtive, I would say. I was very worried cause he looked like he was going down right in front of us.

But here is the miraculous thing. It was some of the best, most creative, brilliant, loose, swinging and sensitive playing I ever heard from him!!! For example, his version of "In Your Own Sweet Way" tells the musical story well. I know Bill's recordings and playing as well as anyone. I think the way he phrased the melody—from the first note of the solo piano intro to the last note—this was fresh Bill!! It was not formulaic. It seemed like at every opportunity Bill was able to make these super creative, unusual, but perfectly logical choices on the spot. Again his rhythmic freedom was astonishing and breathtaking. He seemed to be not just playing the changes but recomposing the tune in each chorus—amazing motivic development for the ages. Bill was somehow able—and this is the crux of it—he was obviously ill, strung out and weak from lack of food, sleep, etc.

His physical condition was terrible. But being the mofo genius musician he was, he could somehow separate his trashed body from the absolute brilliant and creative control of his faculties!! He looked like he was going to fall over, but when he sat at the piano, something took over that was much stronger and resilient than any physical impairment—not only playing ok but he was rolling!! Thriving!! Throwing out stunning ideas with Mozartean-like development. I am not exaggerating. Ask Joe!!

By the way, Joe was incredibly inspiring for Bill because he was able to balance the extreme levels of dynamics that playing in Bill's trio demanded. Also Joe wasn't afraid to throw down with Bill and did not hold back in his intensity and volume—and guess what?? Bill loved it!! He jumped into it. Sometimes in the past, Bill was much more subdued in terms of the range of dynamics he pursued. Not here!! Bill had control over his creativity, control over his chops, time, sound and general presentation.

I wish he had some more control over the paths he chose in other areas of his life. But this trio was fucking alive! Vibrant! Modern! Deep and joyous at times!

This night will forever live in my memory.[3]

Drummer Adam Nussbaum was with Richie Beirach and recalled the night here ...

I went down with Richie Beirach to dig the trio. It was pretty apparent to me that Bill was in rough physical shape. I wondered how he'd be playing. It was difficult to see. Once the music started it was a whole other thing. There was an incredible sense of urgency and creativity that was beyond what I'd heard from him in the past. It was on another level. Looking back, it was like he was looking death in the face and making a final testament breaking through with an unbridled creativity. Marc and Joe were so in there with him. I'll never forget that night.[4]

Pianist Richie Beirach was in the audience for Bill's final performance at Fat Tuesday's in New York City. Richie and Joe had been friends and musical colleagues since their days at Berklee College of Music in Boston. *Photo by David Baker. Courtesy of Richie Beirach.*

It was the same at Keystone Korner the week before where he needed Laurie's help to get on stage. But once seated at the piano, he was transformed—much the same as at a Carnegie Hall gig (where he arrived with his left arm in a cast after an unforeseen car accident; see Appendix). After the Fat Tuesday's gig, we had to carry Bill to the car for the drive home. I had planned on returning to Lake Katrine that night because I had been away from home for several weeks. But seeing how weak Bill was and hoping we could persuade him to go to the hospital, I decided to stay.

Bill lasted two nights. On Thursday, apparently feeling he could drive himself to the gig, he nearly wrecked his car on East Side Highway after nodding off at the wheel. He told Laurie he was unable to play that night, so they took a cab to the club where he explained the situation to Marc and me. Club manager Steve Getz, Stan's son, recruited Andy LaVerne to play the remainder of the week. They brought the audience in, fully expecting

Drummer Adam Nussbaum accompanied Richie Beirach to the same performance at Fat Tuesday's, which turned out to be the last time they saw Bill Evans. *Photo by Adam Nussbaum. Courtesy of Adam Nussbaum.*

to hear Bill Evans. Everybody was seated at their tables. And then Steve made the announcement, "Ladies and gentlemen. We just found out that Bill Evans is unable to play this evening. We're not going to charge a cover. Please stay and listen to Andy LaVerne and Marc and Joe." Each night we repeated the same charade with the audience: Steve got everyone seated and then announced that Bill had suddenly taken ill and would not be able to perform. While people were disappointed, they graciously stayed and seemed to appreciate the music we gave them. Andy did an amazing job under extreme circumstances.

Pianist Andy LaVerne recalled the events of that day …

It was Thursday, September 11, and I had planned to go down to Fat Tuesday's sometime that week and hear Bill. [The late guitarist] John Abercrombie had seen them Wednesday. I was at home in my apartment on W. 23rd St. and playing tunes with bassist Brian Bromberg, who had been working with Stan Getz.

In the late afternoon or early evening, I got a call from Steve Getz, who said, "Bill is sick. We need you to come down and sub." I remember that I told Brian that I just wanted to hang out, relax and play some tunes. And Brian said, "Are you out of your mind?" He admonished me for passing on the chance to sub for Bill Evans and play with Joe and Marc. I took his advice. I didn't leave it to my own discretion. There was no time to prepare. I just grabbed a bunch of my own music … some standards, originals.

The place was jam packed. I thought it would empty out once people knew Bill wasn't playing. It didn't turn out that way. The people were into it. I had a great time playing with Marc and Joe. It was an honor to do the gig. But as you can tell, I didn't think it would be Bill's last gig. I figured they could call somebody else—Richie Beirach, perhaps. I didn't realize the significance of the whole situation.

I can't recall if we played two or three sets. I was still planning on coming down later in the week, and I got a call the following day from Steve. Same story. It happened the same way every night through Sunday. Everyone assumed Bill would be back the next day. Most of us had no idea how sick he was.

While on tour in Switzerland last summer [2018], I met a man who told me he was at Fat Tuesday's on the Thursday night that I played with Joe and Marc. While he was disappointed that Bill wasn't there, he said he really enjoyed the music that evening.[5]

All week long, I gave Bill updates every night when I returned to Fort Lee. And every day, Laurie and I both implored him to see a doctor. At the end of the run on Sunday night, Marc and I went to get paid and were told there was no money left—Bill had drawn it all in advance. A month or so later, after Bill's death, I went to the union's trial board and filed a grievance against Fat Tuesday's and demanded to collect the money for Marc and myself. During that meeting, I said, "Look, I don't know what Bill drew, but our deal with Bill was $750 a week for Marc and myself." And the owner said he gave Bill the money in advance, so he didn't think he owed us at all and, in hindsight, he really didn't. As it turned out, he was a standup guy and paid Marc and me $750 each with the provision that we didn't tell anybody in town. If it got out, he said he wouldn't be able to hire anybody. We were getting double what other players earned in those days.

Andy LaVerne responded to this story …

I wasn't aware that Joe and Marc didn't get paid at the conclusion of the Fat Tuesday's gig. I recall quite clearly that Steve Getz paid me directly at the end of each of the four nights that I subbed for Bill because he assumed that Bill would return the next night. The reason I remember that so well is because Steve told me he was paying me what Bill himself (not the entire trio) was supposed to get each night— $700. I think it was cash, which he got from the bar. That, in part, was the reason I turned down Art Blakey, who came to hear me play with George Mraz at Bradley's shortly after the Fat Tuesday's gig. Art asked me to join the Jazz Messengers and offered a fee of $700 per week (along with traveling in a van). I didn't want to do the gig for that amount after making $700 per night! Not one of my better decisions. What a business![6]

At this very serious point in Bill's life, I was hopeful that he would be admitted to a hospital and somehow recover. That's my nature, I'm afraid—always the optimist but particularly in this case. Denial is a powerful aid in avoiding the truth—even when it was so clearly in front of me. Looking at photos now of Bill from that time reinforced my opinion. It's shocking to see that, in reality, how much he'd physically deteriorated— gaunt, pale, barely eating—while his stellar playing put up a smoke screen of good health.

Chapter 19

September 15, 1980

After the Fat Tuesday's gig closed on Sunday night, I arrived back at the Fort Lee apartment to good news: Bill agreed to see a doctor first thing Monday morning. I was elated and so was Laurie. This was the first time since his health started to seriously deteriorate that he consented to see a physician under any circumstances.

The mood in the apartment was upbeat. Bill lay in bed, so we turned on the television, and there was his longtime friend, John Le Mesurier, the distinguished British actor, in a film. Bill seemed very pleased by this. *Oh look at that. I get to say goodbye to my friend, John Le Mesurier, on the screen there* or something to that effect. He obviously had a firmer grip on his physical situation. I was still in some denial about his health because I actually felt he would somehow survive.

In the morning, Laurie readied Bill for the ride into town as I brought his Chevy Caprice around to the front door. Getting into the car was tough; it was all Bill could do to climb into the backseat and lie down. We headed to Rockefeller University Hospital, where Bill had been treated in a free methadone program. He hoped to speak with his physician and psychiatrist, Dr. Marie Nyswander. But that stop turned out badly. A hospital official turned him away, saying he'd been kicked out of the program due to repeated infractions.

Some 25 years later, I was playing a gig in Los Angeles with pianist Jon Mayer, who told me an interesting story. Turned out that Jon and Bill were in the same rehab program at Rockefeller, which was a complete surprise to me. And Jon saw Bill entering the hospital that morning. Jon fortunately survived his bout with heroin and looks and plays better than ever in Los Angeles. I'll let him tell the rest of the story.

Jon Mayer recalled that day in New York …

Bill's pit stop was to see our mutual doctor, Marie Nyswander, at Rockefeller University Hospital. The methadone treatment program was invented and developed there, and I was in the first outpatient program. Dr. Nyswander was my doctor for years and a very good friend. I had recommended her to Bill years before in the 1970s. By that day in 1980, I was no longer in the program or living in New York. But I wanted to visit with her while in town, and I was in the first floor waiting room opposite the elevators.

I was chatting with Dr. Nyswander and had a view of the elevator banks. I saw Bill as he pressed the button for the second floor for Dr. Nyswander's office, and I said, "There's Bill. I have to say hello."

Apparently, Dr. Nyswander had had some unpleasant experiences with Bill. I'd heard that Bill was messing around with a lot of different things and wasn't doing well. Bill was there to try and talk Dr. Nyswander out of some methadone.

She said to me, "No. Don't say anything." So I sat on my hands and let Bill go up there. Soon after, he came back down and left in a hurry. I never had the conversation I wanted to have that day. I didn't think anything of it. Then within 24 hours, I heard that he died. I just wanted to say hello. I hadn't seen him in years because I wasn't living in New York any longer. I met Bill in 1956 when he first came to New York. He was a very kind and generous guy. I was just this kid piano player that didn't have it wired up at all. I was just learning the form.

> I was absolutely shocked. I heard within a few days there would be a memorial at St. Peters. So I attended it and then went back to Los Angeles.
>
> To this day I have great regrets that I wasn't able to speak with him because he died within 24 hours. I don't know that I would have altered the course of history, but I would have seen him one more time.[1]

Pianist Jon Mayer was a contemporary of Bill Evans. I had worked with Jon for many years in California, and much later in our relationship, we were discussing Bill when Jon told me the same story related in this book (they participated in the same methadone program). *Photo by Bob Barry/Jazzography. Courtesy of Jon Mayer.*

Hearing this so many years after the fact knocked the wind out of me, but I must admit that she was right. No amount of reasoning, begging, cajoling, head butting or anything else was going to prevent this inevitable conclusion to Bill's life. He willed it to happen … and it did. I'm sure that

Helen, Marc and Laurie as well as Dr. Nyswander and many of Bill's other close friends tried in vain to intercede for a long time but to no avail.

After the stop at Rockefeller, we headed uptown to Helen's to pick up $150 that Bill owed me. While stuck in traffic, Bill commented on a very attractive young woman. His exact words were: "I must already be dead because I'm looking at her and I don't feel a thing." Parking was scarce, so I found a spot a block away. Laurie ran around the corner to Helen's. Bill was in no shape to go. Laurie was gone all of ten or fifteen minutes when fate took a hand. As she hopped into the car, Bill started to violently hemorrhage in the backseat. I was 32 years old, a veteran and an Eagle Scout, and I'm telling you, I panicked when I saw him coughing up blood.

Laurie was on the ball, getting Bill to sit upright so he wouldn't choke on his own blood. But Helen's neighborhood was unfamiliar territory for me. Surprisingly, Bill directed me to Mt. Sinai Hospital. In the end, his will to survive at that critical moment overpowered his desire to die. Negotiating the snarled traffic, we came to a railway underpass off Park Avenue that was one way—the wrong way. Bill must have sensed my hesitation and said, "Turn here." I did, my horn blaring, people honking back and cursing. Then it was another turn on to Madison Avenue for the hospital—another one-way street but, again, the wrong way. We managed to arrive at the emergency room entrance and parked.

I mentioned earlier that there were three times when I had to physically hold Bill. This would be the third and final time. I carried him into the hospital, bleeding all over both of us. All I could think of was that he weighed next to nothing. This same man, who only two years ago seemed hale and hearty, was now reduced to skin and bones. I carried Bill to an examination room, and the look in his eyes said it all—I would never see him again.

After getting Bill admitted, I found a phone and called Marc, Helen and my wife. Marc and Helen arrived soon to wait with Laurie and me. It seemed like quite a while before we actually spoke with anyone. But after about an hour, at most, a doctor came out and took Laurie, Helen, Marc and myself into a room where she delivered the bad news: "I'm sorry, but your friend didn't make it."

It's incredible how you can remember a statement like that after all these years, and believe me, when I say for obvious reasons, I don't revisit this particular memory very often. And yet as unpleasant as it was, I would have never forgiven myself if I had not been with Bill at the end. I stayed in New York that entire week instead of going home to my own family because I knew if things went bad, I'd be needed somehow. I loved the man … not just his music.

Helen headed back to her apartment. I drove Marc and Laurie back to Bill's place. Laurie tossed out Bill's drug gear and grabbed her belongings. She gathered up cassettes of the trio from Bill's collection, which Marc and I split between ourselves. I drove back to Lake Katrine, feeling completely wrung out.

Chapter 20

Aftermath
September 1980 to January 1, 1981

The period of time after Bill's death was a mixture of anguish and relief—anguish over Bill's passing and, as heartless or selfish as this may sound, a feeling of relief that it was over. I also experienced an incredible yearning to play with him just one more time. I was negotiating in degrees. I can remember foolishly thinking that I would gladly trade the rest of my life for just one more set! By the end of it, I'd narrowed it down to one more shot at "Nardis." I mean crazy shit like that going through my head, right? Unbelievable madness! The inevitable had happened, and the time for remembering, for mourning and for healing could begin.

The remembering started immediately and continued for two weeks in the form of non-stop phone calls from around the world. People that I knew and many that I did not called with a mixture of concern, condolences and curiosity about what happened. I did not interpret this in any way as morbid because I'm certain that his many friends and acquaintances were simply trying to maintain some kind of contact with Bill—as was I. Many called to wish condolences. Others called to confirm the news and make sure it was not bad gossip. I'm sure it was still fresh news, but even so, once the word had spread that it was confirmed, I still got calls from people. *Can you tell me what happened?* I think they were experiencing the same sense of loss.

Among them was Eddie Gomez who asked about a planned memorial service in New York City. My old friend Rick Petrone, another bass player, also called. Rick hosts a radio show in Stamford, Conn. at the jazz station WYRS, and he wanted to let his listeners know.

Speaking to people and conveying the news was therapeutic and helped me deal with my grief. The memorial service was held Friday, September 19, at St. Peter's Lutheran Church on Manhattan's Upper East Side. Reverend John Garcia Gensel, aka the "Jazz Priest," presided, and the service was broadcast on the Voice of America radio network. Many of Bill's closest friends performed: guitarists Jim Hall and Joe Puma (who recommended me to Bill); saxophonist Lee Konitz; and pianists Richie Beirach and Don Shirley (the concert pianist whose life was profiled in the biopic *Green Book*).

Reverend Gensel read from scriptures, the late jazz critic Nat Hentoff delivered the eulogy, and the service concluded with famed choreographer Carmen de Lavallade performing a modern dance number. Somehow, I managed to play with alto saxophonist Phil Woods in one of three ensembles, but mostly what I remember is openly weeping during the service. As I look over the program today, it's so telling how much respect the jazz world had for Bill. The list of performers is literally a "Who's Who" of greats and many of them long time dear friends like Joe Puma.

Meanwhile, when the phone wasn't ringing—surrounded by my family, Tiffany crawling around on the floor, and my wife at home—I felt more secure. But when they went to bed, I'd stay up late at night. I sat at my electric piano with my headphones on until all hours of the morning playing through Bill's tunes, just trying to grasp on to …. something. I don't know what. I just felt like I needed to do that.

For some time after Bill's death—close to four months—I didn't work. Eventually a few things came along. Some gigs with saxophonists Phil Woods and Zoot Sims. A recording project with pianist Andy LaVerne and Marc on bass. And recordings with trumpeter Tom Harrell and saxophonist

Bill Evans
Memorial Services Program

Friday, September 19, 1980   St. Peter's Lutheran Church   7:30 p.m.

Invocation by Rev. John G. Gensel

Barry Harris: Piano Solo

Group I

Lee Konitz: Sax Solo

Don Shirley: Piano Solo (Two brief compositions)

Joe Puma: Guitar solo

Group II

Jim Hall: Guitar Solo

Group III

Richard Beirach: Piano Solo

Final Dance: Carmen de Lavallade will perform James Weldon Johnson's: "The Creation"

***In addition to the above, there will be scriptures and prayers from
Reverend Gensel. (Speaking will be interspersed between the musical
eulogies as arranged by Rev. Gensel.)
Poetry reading by Bill Zavatsky   Speaker: Nat Hentoff

Musicians' Groups:

Group I	Group II	Group III
Andy LaVerne	Joe La Barbera	Eddie Gomez
Annie Wise	Chuck Israels	Jeremy Steig
Warne Marsh	Phil Woods	Warren Bernhardt
George Mraz	Tom Harrell	Al Foster (?)
	Mike Renzi	

Musicians please note:
The Voice of America will be broadcasting the service. Forms will be
available for you stating the Voice of America tapes will not be used
for commercial purposes.
Thank you, everyone, for giving from yourself in such a beautiful tribute
to the memory of Bill Evans. We are especially grateful to Reverend Gensel
and Eddie Gomez for the memorial service arrangements. —Suzanne Schlunz
                                                        Assistant to Helen Keane

The program for Bill Evans' memorial service at St. Peter's Lutheran Church in Manhattan, four days after his death. *Courtesy of Joe La Barbera.*

Jerry Bergonzi, neither of which were released. Then I got a call from Tony Bennett's office. Butch Miles, Tony's drummer at the time, was leaving. Tony knew Bill well as the two had recorded two albums together. I may have spoken to Tony once at the Village Vanguard when he came in to hear the band. He also showed up at Michael's Pub to hear me with singer Carol Sloane, pianist Jimmy Rowles and bassist George Mraz. And so I took the job, ringing in the new year on my first gig with Tony in Manila.

Chapter 21

Epilogue—Re:
Person I Knew
January 1981 to Present Day

For the next ten years, I toured the world with Tony Bennett, certainly among the best vocalists of all time. After several months of inactivity, the call from Tony's office was a relief, a financial lifesaver to say the least. Tony has always been a favorite singer of mine, and I hoped the job would provide some steady work. In fact, it turned out to be a lot of road time with 220–240 dates a year! During my time with Tony, the gigs ran the gamut from low-paying industrials to many high-profile events—presidential inaugurations in Washington and command performances for British royalty in London. We also encountered royalty of another kind and more meaningful to me: Count Basie, Woody Herman, The Duke Ellington Orchestra directed by Mercer Ellington, Lena Horne, Peggy Lee, Frank Sinatra, Nancy Wilson and Rosemary Clooney. I find it reassuring that Tony is still with us because he's been part of my life since I was five years old.

After working with Tony for a few years, my wife, Carole, and I moved to Phoenix, Ariz. so that we could be closer to her aging parents and her emotionally challenged brother. Our original plan was to spend one year there and then move to Los Angeles, where I could pursue my musical career. In 1983, I rented an apartment in Los Angeles to test the waters, and the first person I reached out to was Shelly Manne, whom I'd met a decade earlier while recording with Chuck Mangione. Our friendship had continued over the years and he was encouraging me to consider relocating there. (Shelly passed in 1984, but I'm still close friends with his widow, Flip.)

But things change, and eventually our marriage deteriorated past any reconciliation. In August of 1987, I packed my drums, my stereo and record collection and headed to L.A. I was still working for Tony Bennett, so I could pay rent, spousal support for a year and child support until Tiffany turned 18. Many players in Los Angeles remembered me from Woody's band, Chuck Mangione and Bill Evans, so I eventually got my foot in the door as a local drummer. Some club dates, weddings (AGAIN!). But I also got to work with some West Coast legends like Conte Candoli, Bud Shank, Bill Perkins and Teddy Edwards. By the time Tony and I parted company in 1993, I had also reconnected with some of my New York city contacts and traveled on tour with them for gigs in Europe.

In January 1993, I took a gig playing a newly commissioned work for an 11-piece band by trombonist Joey Sellers. The performance was in San Antonio, Texas at the International Association for Jazz Education's annual convention. While flying home, I felt a tap on the shoulder from the seat behind me. I looked back to see guitarist Larry Koonse, who wanted to say hello (we'd played a few gigs together). Seated next to him was pianist David Roitstein, chair of the Jazz Studies program at the California Institute of the Arts. Larry, also on faculty there, introduced me to David, who asked if I was interested in teaching at CalArts. Albert "Tootie" Heath was leaving. I jumped at the opportunity to take the job. At the time, I wanted to stay in town so Tiffany could move in with me to attend high school. A brief setback came with the 1994 earthquake in Northridge. Worried by this event, Tiffany and her mom balked at the idea. But she eventually moved out for her senior year, and I was able to enroll her at Hamilton High School, a magnet music and theater school in Culver City. Today, she teaches music at Polytechnic School in Pasadena, plays in an original rock band with her cousins and takes roles in local productions of Broadway musicals.

During my 25-plus years at CalArts, I have occasionally taught a class on Bill Evans in January during a two-week winter session. The class takes a deep dive into Bill over several days. The students are exposed to Bill's early childhood, his first music lessons and eventual discovery of jazz. We follow this trail through college, his first road gig, the U.S. Army and eventual move to New York City where the rest is history. But we listen to a lot of recordings and watch a lot of videos. I have numerous audio clips of Bill that allow him to tell his own story. I also discuss Bill's substance abuse.

For those of us who have never suffered from drug addiction, the idea seems totally foreign. In our minds, we may feel that all one needs to do is face the facts and quit. In reality, it's not so easy. Bill and I discussed this several times and on two occasions, the arguments got heated. My last attempt took place while driving somewhere together midday in Manhattan when he complained about people interfering in his life. He understood that people were concerned about his well-being, but he often, in fact, considered such comments an annoyance. While not singling me out directly, he said he wished that people, though well meaning, would stay out of his personal life. His comment on the subject amounted to *Please don't do me any favors. You have no idea how strong the urge or craving is unless you have it yourself.*

He was certainly right about that, and I'm grateful that I never did. Eventually I came to understand what he was talking about but in a different manner. Over the course of two decades since Bill's passing, I often asked myself *what if?* or *why?* or any number of questions that could put Bill's demons into perspective, and one day it hit me like a ton of bricks. I realized that recovery required not only a desire to stop but also a desire to live on. "You can't talk a man out of a habit unless he really wants to stop," author Ian Carr quotes Miles saying in his excellent book *Miles Davis: The Definitive Biography.*[1] Miles was speaking from personal experience since he had successfully kicked his addiction as did John Coltrane and Sonny Rollins, both former Davis sidemen.

On a few occasions, Bill would speak about making a choice and commitment in regards to jazz. He made that point clear when he turned down singer Tony Martin's generous offer in the 1950s. Also, when asked about someone who may have possessed the talent and intuition of a jazz musician opting for studio work or more lucrative popular styles, Bill would respond without judgment: "He made that choice." When I think of Jon Mayer's comments in Chapter 19, it reminds me that both he and Bill were caught up in substance abuse and both were even seeing the same physician at Rockefeller Center in Manhattan. Thankfully, Jon Mayer chose to live and still makes great music out here in Los Angeles with his trio. I only wish that Bill had made that same choice. "I have probably precisely fulfilled what I had in mind," Bill said in an interview at his alma mater in Louisiana, "which was to attain a position in jazz that would allow me to play what I liked and to have a trio and to record without any pressure."[2] Not many can make that statement at age 51.

I will not begin to try and sort out all the factors that contributed to Bill's death because quite honestly, I don't know all of what was going on in his heart. The obvious red flags would be the two suicides—his first wife, Ellaine Schultz, followed by his brother Harry—and Bill's failing marriage to Nenette. These things alone—combined with an addictive nature and persistent drug abuse of one kind or another—would certainly be enough.

The late composer and journalist Gene Lees famously called Bill's passing "the longest suicide in history."[3] He's not wrong about that. Some part of Bill's personality was attracted to this dark side, and New York had plenty of that.

In a 2001 interview posted online, Bill's widow, Nenette, said he'd been "self-medicating" for decades, and while his struggle with drug abuse experienced peaks and valleys, "in many instances, he surrounded himself with the wrong people ... He should have been hospitalized for drug dependency many times, but he was unable to look at the causes, and when he did seek help in that direction, it was too ineffectual and his illness was too severe."[4]

Regardless of why Bill careened down this road, I would learn during the course of the trio's life that death was not something he feared. We were in New Orleans for a concert at Bill's alma mater, Southeastern Louisiana University, which turned out to be a joyous event for Bill. After sound check, we broke for dinner and to change for the gig. Bill took us to a backwoods-feeling restaurant where the food was supposed to be quite good. About the time we got our meals, a bullet crashed through a nearby window and lodged with a sickening "thud" in a beam literally inches above our heads! Bill saw the alarm in my face and made a crack like *"What's wrong? Are you afraid of dying?"* Well as a matter of fact I was! He may have lost a desire to live, but I had a wife and new baby daughter and most definitely wanted to see them again. And this is when I realized that death was something he was ready to face, that he was not afraid of it.

In an interview with George Klabin about Scott LaFaro, who died at age 25 in a car accident, Bill said, "I can't comprehend death."[5] In Bill's mind, Scott was still here in some way. I don't feel that these were idle words at all because Bill obviously was very intelligent. That he may have never witnessed someone transitioning from life to death may have informed his perspective and, perhaps, this influenced his lifestyle choices. He may have been perfectly willing to die from drug abuse if it was an "on-and-off-switch" kind of experience but not willing to accept diminished capacity as part of the process, especially when it came to performing. Clearly this is conjecture on my part because I'm an armchair psychologist, at best. Bill appeared deeply shaken and frightened after the experience in Italy where he seemed to suffer a cognitive breakdown on stage. I am certain that I saw fear in Bill's eyes on two occasions. Italy was the first, when he struggled to play a song correctly. The second was at Mt. Sinai Hospital when I sat him down in the observation room.

Right after Bill's death, I had this terrible feeling of not only loss but a need for relief. A need to once again recreate the joy we experienced as a band every night. The need I felt so strongly was to play with Bill and Marc again. At times, it seemed overwhelming. Decades later, while teaching my class at CalArts, I realized that what I had been going through back in 1980 was my own form of withdrawal: I was addicted to the music we were making as surely as if it was injected into my arm with a syringe. And there wasn't a pusher on planet earth that could sell me any relief. Under this kind of spell, it was easy to look the other way when Bill's self-destructive behavior threatened his life and the band's success. This may seem completely naive and self-serving, but it's as close to what Bill was feeling as I ever want to get.

Fortunately, my family brought me back to reality. I couldn't imagine ever leaving my beautiful daughter or causing any heartache to my wife. One of my big regrets, looking back now, is that Bill missed out on having a relationship with his children—his son, Evan, an intelligent, articulate and motivated young man with a successful career composing for movies and TV; and Maxine, his stepdaughter who has become a success in her own right as a photographer who I know Bill loved dearly.

Since that time (and time does heal), I have rediscovered over and over the pure joy of playing music with great musicians. Every jazz musician strives for the best possible performance and communication. This makes playing a joy. Bill Evans played a significant part in my musical life from early teens up to the present. Those special moments playing music that occur where something resonates so deeply that you never forget it are extremely rare. Hearing Bill on record for the first time was one such moment, and every one of his recordings after that added to the feeling. By the time I actually climbed on the stage with him in 1979, he felt like an old musical friend. It was definitely a challenge but welcoming at the same time. As Bill, Marc and I forged a deep musical closeness, it also became personal—like any friend, you become concerned for their well-being. The Bill I met at Hopper's in 1978 was much more robust than the man who deteriorated daily before my eyes. But the energy and urgency of his playing greatly belied the physical reality of his health.

I wanted Bill to live, and I wanted the trio to grow as much as possible. This may be considered a selfish point of view, but it's what I was hoping for. In the end, it didn't happen. Many years later when I think of Bill, it's always a happy memory. The things I learned on the bandstand with him, I now pass along to anyone I play with, whether a student or pro: Full commitment to the music without distraction; trying to elevate your audience while never playing down to them; always having an ear to everyone else and being there to help out when needed. I don't "flip a switch" as Bill used to say but once the music starts, I allow it to take over and I trust my instincts to react.

I'm getting better at it.

Appendix

Sorrow in Soho
by François Lacharme

The photograph was taken in one-thirtieth of a second in December 1979 in Bordeaux. I had wedged the old Zenith between two folders, facing the stage of Théâtre Fémina. A greenish iridescence gave a catafalque-like look to the grain of the enlargement. A few hours more by train and then a ferry crossing, and it would be hand-delivered to the dedicatee. This atmospheric shot was the pretext for meeting Bill Evans at Ronnie Scott's. My father and I hesitated for a long time on the attached note. But how to dedicate to the attention of the one who usually dedicates? This dilemma kept us pondering for a long time. Then the kraft envelope closed on this irresolute safe-conduct. "One quid, guv'nor!" The London taxis don't avoid direct routes, and they drop off at the right place. The entrance of the Frith Street club is cozy, with that *je-ne-sais-quoi* uniformity that betrays cosmopolitan pretension. Some spots erase the solemn carpet of the place. To the right, a vitrine is there where some souvenirs certify to the layman that the jewels are never very far from the crown. Among these objects, there is an original portrait of the series of drawings that served to illustrate the LP envelope of Bill Evans' *New Conversations*. The presence of this work gave me the impression that one could judge it of a doubtful augury.

Facing Death

Catherine R., who triumphed over her inaccessibility to complex chords through a beautiful plasticity of mind and body, pulls me by the sleeve. The table for two that I had reserved happens to be the first in the axis of the keyboard. In extending the arm, we titillate the last octave. The voice-over, like always at Ronnie Scott's, announces the trio as they enter the stage. Dressed in an unremarkable chestnut brown, Joe La Barbera, Marc Johnson and Bill Evans—who walks with difficulty—rejoin their instruments.

The Bill Evans Trio on stage in Bordeaux, France. French journalist François Lacharme brought this photo to Bill later at a performance at Ronnie Scott's Jazz Club in London. Taken from the audience using the available light, Lacharme always felt the photo had important historical and sentimental value. *Photo by François Lacharme. Courtesy of François Lacharme.*

The glasses keep silent. The quality of the silence that precedes the first notes is dizzying, and one would hardly suspect that a tempo was given. It would be an understatement to say that what followed was for me a revelation. Bill Evans forces us to rethink his music: hierarchies crumble, the very story that shaped his style is diluted in an outburst that capsizes the soul. All that we had patiently constructed to take the place of a dialectic is suddenly reduced to a murky idea in which sufferings, magnificently impossible loves, chords excavated and then elucidated, bodies in perdition, all collide. How many subterfuges of facing death in order to achieve the violence of this emotion? One would have to believe in a pharisaic definition of music to believe that Bill Evans does not put his life before our eyes.

Two Fateful Notes

I remember the compositions. There was "Laurie," from his last quintet album (*We Will Meet Again*) that had just been released and "Bill's Hit Tune," also from the same LP, two themes less fortunate than others for their exclusion from the Real Book (unlike, for example, "Waltz for Debby"). Finally, the set concludes with "My Romance" that he adorned again with a monumental introduction—giving the illusion that the emotional charge will be calmed while moving on popular ground, but even "Days of Wine and Roses" or "Like Someone in Love" belied this gravity behind a smiling facade. The trio played "Letter to Evan" (dedicated to his son), a confession that he frequently made public. And then this theme that only Bill Evans could write, a ground flight for new harmonic heavens, "Knit For Mary F." Sitting within earshot of the pianist, I whisper "Nardis!" at the end of the set. In hindsight, it was cheeky. But the other voices approve. Bill Evans turns for a long time around the two fateful notes without even taking the time to glance toward his partners.

Rhythmic Harmony

Should we then rewrite the history that everyone knows? Dare to scratch behind the icon: Bill Evans' last concerts contradict the rather stable image that the observers usually describe, where the refined and sometimes bold harmonist, the "dialogist" instituting the equilaterality of his musical triangle, and the introverted lyricist dominate. That night, even more radically than eight months before in Bordeaux, I heard the pianist leave the efflorescence of impressionism to find the taut arch, the distraught poetry of the last quartets of Beethoven, the illuminated rage of Chopin's Sixth Polonaise. I heard him powerfully engage the keyboard, hands close together, pressing the metronome through this "rhythmic harmony" that sometimes sharply anticipated the measure, giving the perfect illusion that each one of them was attracted by the next. The nuances of touch were sacrificed; he was playing into the piano—that of Ronnie Scott's was very tired—as if by force. I then understood that this "all-in," put on the chopping block of thirty 30 years of work, could not have materialized without the measured savagery of Marc Johnson's playing. One will object, and rightly so, that I am biased. But his bass lines that night (and some others to which the record bears witness) put him a notch above the most exalted dreams of complicity that the pianist had with Scott La Faro, Eddie Gomez or, for a short time, Gary Peacock, to name only the most emancipated. [Francis Paudras was present at least twice during this concert series at Ronnie Scott's. I was too young to know him. He (or one of his friends) recorded at least the first and the last night, published for a few months under a double CD at Dreyfus Jazz under the names of Bill Evans Trio, *Turn Out the Stars/Live at Ronnie Scott's* and *Letter to Evan/Live at Ronnie Scott's*. Both are no longer in circulation.]

Few contrabassists at the time concentrated so many qualities *forcing* the music to advance: agile but precise, creating a profusion of rhythmic accidents that punctuated the swing of a youth serum, nuancing the chronometer with minuscule accelerations, outlining the pianist's endemic left hand with a leaping contrapuntal idea. His lyricism was already bound by the bit of a beautifully connected brain. Joe La Barbera told me recently about the creative arc of this young lion, just out of Woody Herman's band and enthusiastically accepted by "Philly" Joe Jones, and still in full development. [When Marc Johnson came to replace Chuck Israels with Bill Evans for the last set in a New York club in '78, "Philly"

ronnie scott's

47 Frith Street, West One. Tel. 439·0747

Mon May 19th for 2 weeks

L A 4
RAY BROWN   BUD SHANK
LAURINDO ALMEIDA JEFF HAMILTON
& RONNIE SCOTT QUARTET

Mon June 2nd for 2 weeks
BUDDY DeFRANCO
TERRY GIBBS QUINTET
& RONNIE SCOTT QUARTET

Mon June 16th for 2 weeks
ART PEPPER
QUARTET

Mon June 30th for 1 week
CHICO HAMILTON
QUINTET

Mon July 7th for 2 weeks
JOE PASS with
NIELS PEDERSEN

Mon July 21st for 2 weeks
BILL EVANS TRIO

Mon Aug 4th for 2 weeks

DIZZY GILLESPIE
QUARTET

Mon Aug 18th for 2 weeks
YUSEF LATEEF
QUINTET

*If you would like to send your friends greetings from Ronnie Scotts Club.
Ask a Waiter or Waitress or Door Staff for one of our postcards; fill it in and
we will send it anywhere in the World for you — post free!*

PLEASE TELEPHONE FOR RESERVATIONS AND FURTHER DETAILS.
The Management reserves the right to alter the Programme.

The program from Ronnie Scott's on the night François Lacharme attended a performance by the Bill Evans Trio. *Courtesy of François Lacharme.*

Joe Jones (who was part of the trio at the time) was all smiles as he looked at the pianist: "We have our new bassist!" His words possessed the promise of a contract.] In the case of the "triangular triangle," we can wonder if it is not especially between the pianist and his contrabassist that the musical coupling occurred. But to see in Joe La Barbera (who also passed through Herman's band) only an attentive candleholder is to be deaf to these imperceptible signals that circulated between the drummer and the pianist, like seams that hide the rectitude of a perfectly smooth piping. The evenings at Ronnie Scott's revealed to me a drummer with the reflexes of a *chamber music player*: He knew how to play strong even when playing quiet.

Thirty years and hundreds of grieving listens have passed since that moment, when at the end of the concert, leaning his waxen face over the envelope containing the photograph, he took the time to read the dedication whose generous aplomb hid the epigrammatic meaning too well: "From a lifetime admirer." He thanked me in such a soft voice that I could see how weak he was and possibly close to death. I was 19 years old and felt that so strongly and so emotionally close to his music that, metaphorically, I was ready to leave this earth with him.

This story was translated from the original by Jordan Fox with additional editing by François Lacharme, Charles Levin, and Joe La Barbera. It first appeared in the French publication *Jazz Magazine* in October 2010 and appears with permission of the author.

Essays by Joe La Barbera

Similarities

In looking at Bill's life and my own, I discovered quite a few similarities, which may have contributed to the ease of our musical and personal relationship. Bill started lessons at an early age as did I—6 for Bill, 5 for me. Bill had an older brother, Harry, who was also keenly interested in music and jazz, in particular, and was also a huge influence. I have two older brothers—Pat and John—and to this day, we all share a passion for jazz. I have looked up to and learned from them my entire life. Bill's family played and sang together often and this was his introduction to music. Along with our parents, we performed as a family band for over a decade.

Bill worked with older musicians who were very patient and helpful to his growth when he was in his teens. I did the same all through high school, working with a variety of local musicians, ranging in age from mid-30s to mid-60s. They were all very helpful to me in every way, including providing rides to and from gigs. Stylistically, Bill and I played a lot of the same music from polkas to swing era standards to the popular music of the day. In Bill's case, this would have been the 1940s, in mine, the 1950s.

Bill was a Boy Scout, achieving the rank of Life Scout. My brothers and I all became Eagle Scouts, thanks to the hard work and participation of our parents. Marc Johnson once told me that Bill was impressed with this fact. What can I say?

Bill completed his formal studies in 1950, earning a bachelor's degree in piano performance and teaching from Southeastern Louisiana University. He also spent three semesters in graduate school at Mannes School of Music in Manhattan (now part of The New School). I attended Berklee College of Music in Boston, but left after three semesters to play gigs on the road. Bill played in the Herbie Fields Big Band for almost a year after college before joining the Army. I joined Woody Herman's Band for a year after my military service.

We both served in the U.S. Army during wartime but managed to stay stateside in a post band. Bill played in the 5th Army Headquarters Band at Fort Sheridan in Chicago from 1951 to 1954, and I served in the 173rd Army Band at Fort Dix, New Jersey from November 4, 1968 to November 5, 1970. We would occasionally share stories from our past and compare notes. For example, both of us made E-5 in rank (sergeant), and neither one of us particularly enjoyed the service.

In 1955, Bill moved to New York with about $150 in his pocket, but confident he would find work. I moved to New York in 1976 with about $1,000 and hopeful I could at least get some club dates or weddings to survive. Things started to happen fairly quickly for Bill, and he soon found work as a sideman for Tony Scott, George Russell and Mundell Lowe. I was lucky, too, and soon got gigs with guitarists Jim Hall, Joe Puma, Gene Bertoncini and Jack Wilkins as well as vibraphonist Gary Burton, saxophonists Joe Farrell and Michael Brecker, trombonist Bob Brookmeyer and harmonica virtuoso Toots Thielemans.

Like Bill, I also played weddings and casuals (private parties). He used to say his tux was always pressed and ready for any occasion! So was mine! I used to play weddings with an accordion player and tenor sax player in between Bill's gigs to pay the rent.

I mention all of this because it directly affected the relationship Bill and I had, which was more fraternal than the father-son relationship I felt he had with Marc. The fact that I was closer in age to him and had more experience under my belt at the time also factored in somewhat.

But here is where the similarities end because I view Bill as a true giant in the world of jazz. His playing, his trio concepts, his compositions are all original; they're all his own. Gary Burton once told me during a long van ride that one of the measures of a great artist is the number of hopefuls that he or she inspires. I would have to agree with that definition and in Bill's case it can be magnified exponentially because among the "hopefuls" that he influenced you can include Herbie Hancock, Chick Corea and Keith Jarrett, who all went on to become true giants.

I am not being overly self-effacing when I say that I know that I can play and that I have something of my own but nowhere near the level of creative ideas or sphere of influence in any direction that Bill possessed.

***

Historical Perspective

When it comes to Bill Evans, fans and musicians alike all have their favorite trios and eras of Bill's career. Bill would never compare trios "qualitatively but more in terms of spirit" as he stated in an interview after a concert in Molde, Norway.[1] Certainly, reasonable minds can argue the talents and abilities of the individual members of each trio. I would not fare too well in a side-by-side with "Philly" Joe Jones, who, by anyone's estimation, including my own, was one of the greatest jazz drummers of all time—and Bill's personal favorite, I might add.

The fact is, all of Bill's trios were great and for a very simple reason: Bill Evans was the pianist in each one. Arguably, the bassists and drummers who played with Bill were all exceptional and made enormous contributions to his music and musical growth. Bill's intense emotional style, self-expression, clarity of thought and overall extremely high musicianship can be experienced on *all* of his recordings, no matter who his partners were.

Bill Evans raised each one of us to a level only he could help us achieve, and this informed the musical journey we experienced later in our careers. Some musicians have this ability and strength to lift everyone around them. Bill had this quality ... in spades. He gave me the strength that allows me to help other musicians play their best. Besides being a great soloist, Bill was an equally great accompanist, always listening and supportive to the soloist. For me, this aspect of being a musician, particularly in the rhythm section, is as enjoyable as taking a solo.

I feel there's a misconception regarding Bill Evans' preference for sidemen. Bill stayed open to working with players from a variety of styles and interests. As I've said before, "Philly" Joe Jones was his all-time favorite drummer and obviously Bill felt a very special connection with bassist Scott LaFaro, especially in the development of the trio's identity. But the first bass player he hired for his trio was Jimmy Garrison and, of course, he worked with Paul Chambers in Miles Davis' band. Bill told me that he always enjoyed playing with Percy Heath and, on one occasion at the Village Vanguard, bassist John Clayton sat in, and Bill enjoyed that as well.

That all the trios had merit in their own way was not lost on jazz journalists, critics or fans.

The trio with bassist Scott LaFaro and drummer Paul Motian was the genesis of a concept that grew naturally out of a commitment and a desire to create something personal in the music. For me and for legions of Bill Evans fans, this group represents the pinnacle of that goal, and I think that we can stipulate right here and now that these three musicians created something entirely new that the rest of us have been able to follow.

Bassist Chuck Israels played in trios with drummers Motian, Larry Bunker and Arnold Wise, all to high praise from the press. *Moonbeams,*

How My Heart Sings and *Bill Evans Trio with Symphony Orchestra* are classic recordings featuring these trios. The group with bassist Chuck Israels and Wise was short lived but produced one of his finest recordings, *Bill Evans at Town Hall.* Jim Franksen, writing in the October 1967 issue of *Jazz and Pop*, said, "The trio section is elegant also. Chuck Israels has progressed well in his playing in Evans' trio. It's hard to imagine a more beautiful meshing of musical thought and ideas. Arnold Wise is one of three single drummers who did well with Bill. Hats off to these two fine and sympathetic musicians."[2]

The group featuring bassist Eddie Gomez and drummer Marty Morell drew similar kudos. "I doubt that Evans will ever disband this trio, for it's one of the most sensitive, responsive, vital groupings in jazz," according to a December 1974 *DownBeat* review of *The Tokyo Concert*. "Hearing this group in person has always given me the sensation that these three musicians' minds have somehow fused into one collective consciousness."[3]

Ditto for the pairing of Gomez and drummer Jack DeJohnette. "It is immediately evident from the intricate, free, but never intrusive drummer's counterpoint of Jack DeJohnette ... and from the interplay with Evans of bassist Eddie Gomez ... that this is a trio of virtual equals ... and the best ensemble Evans has had in some time," Martin Williams wrote in the *New York Times* in January 1969 of the recording *Bill Evans at the Montreux Jazz Festival.*[4]

And the compliments poured in, yet again, when Bill teamed Gomez with drummer Eliot Zigmund. "Bill Evans was as great as ever ...," said Michael Bourne in an October 1976 issue of *Radio Free Jazz*. "The spirited and spiritual interplay of the trio was almost awesome. And it's always a music within the musicians. They never talk, except through the music."[5]

Our trio was drawing a younger audience, and their enthusiasm was contagious. Historically, Bill Evans never concerned himself with audience reaction and certainly was never bothered by the fact that most of his solos might go unacknowledged by applause. He told me that he would actually tailor his solos dynamically to end at a point which would allow the bass solo to begin without interruption. However, this changed noticeably during one of our week-long engagements at the Vanguard. Bill was energized, and at the conclusion of his solo on "Someday My Prince Will Come," the audience exploded with an ovation. I remember looking directly at him and the absolute surprise on his face. He commented later, almost to the point of

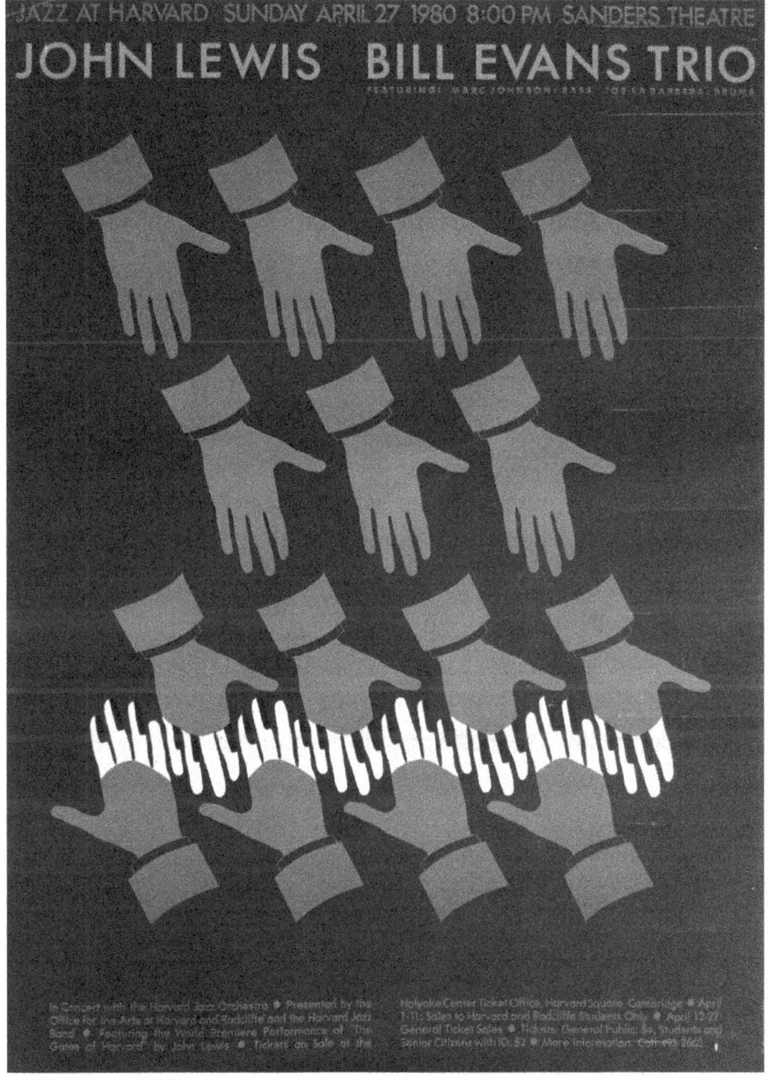

A poster for a rare duo performance on April 27, 1980 at Harvard University by Bill Evans and pianist John Lewis of the Modern Jazz Quartet. *Courtesy of Joe La Barbera.*

embarrassment, *Man, that's never happened before*. But this would happen more and more going forward.

Meanwhile, Bill weighed in with this comment about the trio with Marc and myself. "I have the feeling that this current trio is more similar to the one with Scott and Paul than any I've had before," he told Robert Kenselaar in a 1979 interview in *The Aquarian*. "I don't know how, exactly, what it is except that they inspire me to go for that fresh approach and when I do, they go right with whatever is happening. Maybe it's the mixture of personalities and interests. I don't want to put down any of the trios that I've had because they're all special in their own way. But I feel like the perspective for this trio offers some potential that the others might not have had."[6]

Robert Palmer, writing in a 1979 *Rolling Stone* interview, agreed. "Johnson and La Barbera are sensitive and adept musicians," Palmer wrote. "They aren't the most spectacular virtuosos on their instruments. But they are the right players ... right for Evans."[7]

The point here is that Bill had no agenda for a new member of the trio other than keep your ears open and respect the music. What's really important to me in all these comments is that this is what Bill was feeling. Fans and history will decide who they like the best; it's really not the point. I'd be happy if my epitaph read, "Bill Dug Me."

In the two years I played with him, he never put his own ego ahead of the music. As a sideman, I was given a great deal of freedom but along with it came responsibility. The music came first—always.

***

From the Listeners' Ears

After years of experience performing in public, I have come to embrace the comments I receive from audience members who precede their statement with something like, "I don't really know anything about jazz, but I just want to say..."

Obviously not all of these comments are keepers ("Do drummers read music?"). But there have been many where an uninitiated listener with a willingness to *fully participate* in the music has summed up—in lay terms—exactly what we played and always strived for. As far as I'm concerned, that's the ultimate in musical communication.

The farmer who spoke with Marc Johnson on the break at Rick's Café Americain in Chicago is a perfect example. This man came in for a drink in the hotel bar where he was staying and was drawn into a style of music he was unfamiliar with. By the time the set ended, he heard music on a level he had never experienced before.

Another comes from the essay written by François Lacharme, titled *Sorrow in Soho,* where he described his second live encounter with Bill Evans' music at Ronnie Scott's in London. Lacharme, who was only 19 at the time, made some wonderful observations that I would like to delve into a bit for the uninitiated listener.

His vivid description of entering Ronnie Scott's brought back to mind my very first visit to New York City in 1962. Joined by my older brothers, I was 14 and walking down the steps near the corner of Broadway and 52nd Street into Birdland. I can literally *see* the inside of the club in my mind's eye and, of course, the music played by Dizzy Gillespie's Quintet left a lasting impression.

While François's descriptions of the interior of Ronnie Scott's are spot on, it's his musical insights I find the most intriguing. He describes his date, Catherine, as someone "who triumphed over her inaccessibility to complex chords through a beautiful plasticity of mind..."[8] This *plasticity of mind* is exactly what I refer to above as a willingness to *fully participate* in the music. The silence that preceded the music was always the same because Bill never said a word in advance to the audience or to us. We all waited for the first sounds to emerge from the piano and then it began. Bill Evans forced you to rethink his music because it was ever-evolving and would always include everything he and the band had experienced. Elvin Jones, among others, once stated that you should play as if it was the last time in your life. Bill did that every night.

François' recollection of the repertoire is accurate as compared with the music included in the two CDs that subsequently came out years later (*Letter to Evan* Dreyfus 191-064-2 and *Turn Out the Stars* Dreyfus 191-063-2).

Now we get the really good stuff!

Bill worked long and hard on his concept of melodic and harmonic displacement, making it sound natural, flowing and easy to do—but it's not. Yes, anyone can anticipate a chord in advance of the next measure, but to do this across entire phrases and make complete musical sense with your ideas and form them into a cohesive solo is miraculous! François describes poetically and artistically this approach that took Bill a long time to perfect: "... this 'rhythmic harmony' that sometimes sharply anticipated the measure, giving the perfect illusion that each one of them was attracted by the next."

If you are interested, I recommend that you listen to the episode that Bill recorded with the late Marian McPartland on her NPR program, *Piano Jazz*, which originally aired on November 6, 1978. Marian, who was a fine jazz pianist, asked Bill about the displacement approach, and Bill demonstrated beautifully on the standard tune "All of You." After Bill concluded, Marian commented that she was trying to jump in with a bass line but was completely lost. This is understandable for anyone who is unaware of the process and has at least some experience with it.

But what exactly does all this mean to a listener who simply wants to be entertained? It's a feeling of being a bit off balance but at the same time completely trusts that the musicians will land you safely in your chair at the end.

And Bill always did.

***

Reflections on Bill

Over forty years have elapsed since Bill Evans' death. Since that time a day hasn't passed without his memory being evoked in some way in my life. Whether through music, family life or even exercise (unbelievable!), I am reminded of him in different ways. I realize that Bill Evans and exercise don't automatically equate in most jazz fans' minds, but he was in fact a very athletic youth, who played par golf, was a scratch bowler and a pool shark!

The reason he comes to my mind when I'm jogging is from a silly statement he made as a mild jibe to me regarding his fitness routine: "Two rollovers in bed each night with a brisk walk to the bathroom!"

He craved a normal family life and was always concerned about how mine was holding up with all the travel involved with the trio.

Most often, of course, he comes to mind with music. The many lessons I learned from him have stayed with me and shaped my musical life in a significant way. Just being on stage with him had a transforming effect. He was completely committed to the music, immersed from the minute we started to perform. The music grew from song to song in an organic and dynamic way each night but always guided by a clear vision of a complete and satisfying program. I have learned from every bandleader I have ever worked for from Gap Mangione to Woody Herman to Chuck Mangione to Bill and Tony Bennett. They all had a great sense for programming a set of music, so that both the audience and players left happy.

Beyond this fundamental point, they all believed in what they were playing, which is crucial to making music. Woody told me once to "be careful what you become famous for because you will end up playing it every night for the rest of your life." This was, I thought, a tongue in cheek reference to "Woodchopper's Ball," which was the least favorite tune among the younger guys in the band, but was, in fact, for the song "Laura," a vocal hit for Woody early on. Tony Bennett would never sing any song he didn't absolutely love. And he makes each performance sound as if it were not only the first time he's sung it, but that he is singing it just for you!

An interviewer once asked Bill if the reason he played many standard songs was so that his audience would recognize them. Bill was actually surprised by this question and said he had never thought about it in that way. He even took it a step further since the implication was that he was somehow manipulating his audience, to say that if he wanted to go that route he was certainly intelligent enough to analyze what makes a successful song and come up with a formula for success. He felt that people who know and like standard tunes don't necessarily like jazz and would probably prefer to hear them done in a Muzak style instead. He only played songs he liked and would find them everywhere.

Many of the best composers in the world were fans of Bill's and would send their songs to him. I can remember seeing originals by Johnny Mandel, Alan and Marilyn Bergman, and Michel Legrand on Bill's piano, and I can also remember speaking with Mandel on the phone one afternoon when I was staying with Bill. The tune "Minha" came from the great Brazilian composer Luis Eça. I had the pleasure of hearing Bill play that song live when he sat in at a club where Eça performed solo piano on Ipanema Beach in Rio De Janeiro to the great delight of all. I'm not certain how Bill found "Jesus' Last Ballad" by Italian musician Gianni Bedori but it is a gem. Other gems by Gary McFarland, Steve Swallow, Joe Zawinul, and Denny Zeitlin made their way into the trio's repertoire and received special care in Bill Evans' hands. And, of course, Earl Zindars' compositions were a staple of our repertoire. Bill always maintained a balance between the Great American Songbook, originals by the aforementioned composers and his own compositions.

What this tells all of us is that Bill was completely dedicated to his art in a way that only a few have been in jazz. Monk, Miles and Coltrane come immediately to mind. We are all the beneficiaries of the dedication of these great artists.

***

Roots of the Trio

The Bill Evans Trio with Scott LaFaro and Paul Motian broke new ground in the world of jazz. Three different voices—piano, bass, drums—interacted seamlessly in a highly creative and rhythmically freer manner while still adhering to an established song form; it was revolutionary. Today, it's a more standard approach, adopted by many musicians, particularly in the piano trio format. It took the combination of these three minds coming together with a willingness for exploration and a commitment to a group at a time when jazz was once again undergoing a transformation.

Drummer Paul Motian was a protégé of the great Max Roach, whose playing, early on, he emulated. This can be heard on early recordings, like Bill's first trio date on Riverside, *New Jazz Conceptions*. Much of the language Paul used in his comping and soloing came directly from Max and reflected the status quo of the *Post-Bop* sound. Middle Eastern and Turkish music from his parents' record collection and Armenian Church music also informed Paul's drumming. Before joining Bill Evans' trio, Paul worked with

Thelonious Monk, Lennie Tristano and Tony Scott, so his ears and intellect were already in tune with something different. All three men defied categorial norms and blazed uncharted territory in jazz. When you look at the artists Paul played with *post-Evans*, you can hear that he always searched for new expressions of the music.

Although a latecomer to the upright bass, Scott LaFaro followed a rapid trajectory of growth that required endless hours of dedicated practice in not only the basic techniques of the bass but in the traditional *straight ahead* swinging approach to playing the music. His legacy of recorded work in this style is limited but more than adequate to confirm that he could walk with the best of them at any tempo. For example, on *The Arrival of Victor Feldman*, the tempo on Dizzy Gillespie's tune, "Bebop," is a blistering 400 beats per minute, and Scott never wavers even though drummer Stan Levey *strolls* (lays out) for the "A" sections.

The next track, "There is No Greater Love," takes a much more relaxed pace and displays Scott's big tone and full, swinging feel. Similar recordings with Hampton Hawes (*For Real!*) and Stan Getz (*Stan Getz and Cal Tjader*) show Scott as a musician in full control of his skills. After arriving in New York, Scott discovered the music of Eric Dolphy and other *free* jazz players for which he had an affinity as well. Two worlds colliding? In an interview by Martin Williams in *DownBeat* dated August 1960, Scott comments on his approach this way: "My ideas are so different from what is generally acceptable nowadays that I sometimes wonder if I am a jazz musician. I remember that Bill and I used to reassure each other some nights kiddingly that we really were jazz musicians."[9]

Bill Evans was very well versed in earlier styles, having spent more time on his chosen instrument than Scott (who took up the bass after a career-ending basketball accident took out his clarinet embouchure forever). Evans played *stride*, *swing* and *be-bop* with assuredness, but his heart was not really into the status quo *hard bop* or *avant-garde* of the late 1950s. Case in point is that he held the piano chair in the greatest jazz band of that time, The Miles Davis Sextet, and gave notice after nine months. He was hearing something else. Bill's roots in jazz ran very deep. As documented in an interview with John Mehegan in *Jazz Magazine*, Bill said, "Oh sure, my first playing was boogie-woogie, influenced by Pete Johnson and Albert Ammons. And I heard pianists all over the country in my work from New Orleans Dixieland through Chicago—Art Hodes, for instance; Earl Hines, Nat Cole, Teddy Wilson—everybody I ever heard, including yourself."[10] This describes Bill Evans to a "T."

In an early interview with Nat Hentoff from *DownBeat* magazine in the October 1959 issue, Bill spoke of his desire to seek more freedom with the music: "I want to be able to be free to go in my own direction without having to drag other people into my way of thinking. Ideally, I'd like to play solo piano but from a practical standpoint, in terms of establishing a reputation and the kinds of rooms one can play, a trio makes more sense. I'm hoping the trio will grow in the direction of simultaneous improvisation rather than just one guy blowing followed by another guy blowing."[11]

These words were spoken just after the inception of the trio with Scott and Paul and following the Riverside album *Everybody Digs Bill Evans,* a title that caused great embarrassment for Bill. The first trio was actually bassist Jimmy Garrison and drummer Kenny Dennis, assembled for an ill-fated engagement at Basin Street East opposite Benny Goodman. Conditions for the trio were so bad that seven different bass players and four different drummers quit the job. The end result was, in fact, the trio with Scott and Paul.

Kenny and I have been friends since I moved to Los Angeles, and we share the distinction of being the first and last drummers in Bill's trios. Kenny told me that during this gig, Bill asked him to "play against me sometimes," a direction that most drummers would find confusing since we are trained to work *with* other musicians. Perhaps Bill just hadn't formulated the words to express this freedom of movement that he was seeking. In hindsight, most drummers today at least understand conceptually what Bill was asking and many use this approach as a way of creating tension for release at a later point in the music.

What Bill Evans was seeking musically and what he found in the trio with Scott and Paul was not only two very capable musicians but musicians who made a commitment to a group and the necessary sacrifices for the music and the trio's success. In another interview with Don Nelson from *DownBeat*, December 8, 1960, Bill stated: "As a leader, it's my role to give direction to the group ... and Paul and Scott have indicated that they are more comfortable in the group than anywhere else."[12]

The rapid growth within this trio and the music itself is testimony to that commitment.

***

Regarding New Music

"I'm not foolish enough to think that I can go to a teacher to learn how to communicate."

—Bill Evans, DownBeat, November 22, 1962[13]

"I had to work harder at music than most cats because you see, man, I don't have very much talent. But it's true. Everybody talks about my harmonic conception. I worked very hard at that because I didn't have very good ears. Maybe working at it *is* the talent."

—Bill Evans, The Gene Lees JazzLetter, 1984.[14]

By early 1980, a lot of new music was finding its way into the trio's book. I think "Letter to Evan" came first and is as personal a statement as Bill ever made in music. By this time, he seemed aware that he would not be around to watch his only child, Evan, grow up and the song reflects remorse combined with fatherly love and hope for the future. Like most new songs, Bill just started playing it on the gig, and we would work out what fit and what didn't. I eventually opted to lay out on this one for a few reasons. First of all, I just couldn't find a different way to express the time feel to differentiate it from other walking ballads. Secondly, it always worked with Marc joining Bill on the second chorus, and the two of them were complete in every way. Finally, where Bill placed it in the set was a logical spot for the drums to disappear for a while. Usually the next tune in the set had some heat so, all in all, it just made sense to me.

"Tiffany," the song Bill wrote for my daughter, came next due to her arrival in this world on February 29, 1980. I have a feeling that Bill gave this arrangement some thought before bringing it to the bandstand because it was fully formed with an introduction and very hip ending right from the start. Bill also introduced "Laurie," a dedication to Laurie Verchomin, around this time—a thoughtful and loving tribute to a very special woman. "Yet Ne'er Broken" (originally titled "Out of the Blue") and "Knit For Mary F," followed, and we played all of these in the weeks leading up to the record dates at the Village Vanguard during the first week of June 1980. Bill had been working on "Knit For Mary F" during the time that I was staying with him because I would hear him play it during the day sometimes.

Historically, as previously stated, Bill was well organized and logical with the repertoire. In 1980, CBC interviewer Ross Porter (Canadian Broadcasting Corp.) asked Bill why he played standards, suggesting he did it because most audiences could more easily relate to this material. Bill's response was illuminating to say the least. First off, he said that he only played what he liked, and it never occurred to him that this tactic would help him build up his fan base. And if he took that approach, he told Porter, he was certainly intelligent enough to analyze enough data to come up with a strategy that would allow him to pick the right material for economic success. He also added that people who like standards don't necessarily like jazz and may prefer to hear someone like Mantovani play their favorites. Classic Bill. He would never use a tactic like that to attract fans. He concentrated his energies on the music and preparation of a song for performance.[15]

We once discussed his approach to formatting a piece of music for the trio. Here's the process as Bill explained it to me: Pick the tune, pick the key, pick the tempo, figure out any harmonic substitutions and then create the arrangement. Once all of this is set, it actually frees the musicians up to focus totally on creativity. If you look over Bill's repertoire from the first recording to the last, you will find a consistency in performances of the arrangements with only subtle variations to the set chart. The improvised solos are all different.

In one case, Bill selected the tune, "My Foolish Heart." Here's an example that was actually documented in audio and released by George Klabin on the CD *Pieces of Jade* on Resonance Records.[16] The tune is a theme from a film, *My Foolish Heart*, which starred Dana Andrews and Susan Hayward. As Scott tunes up, Bill starts playing the tune in the key of E, which may be from the original sheet music. He moves from E to F and Scott joins in, but they gradually change to A which favors Scott because it allows him to use the open E and A strings to great advantage. They work out specific chord substitutions for several minutes that involve a lot of trial and error when Bill decides that the tempo is too fast; he slows it down.

The back and forth dialogue between Bill and Scott is fascinating, and I have transcribed the entire text for my class but you may find all of this boring or uninteresting and that is totally fine because it's not your job to worry about the details that go into a performance. You get to enjoy the fruits of the artists' labor unencumbered.

My point is that the roughly twenty minutes that these two artists spent working out the finer points of the arrangement resulted in one of the most incredible performances of a ballad ever on record! By knowing in advance the framework they would work with, the trio was liberated to express it. Paul Motian's use of the sizzle cymbal (with rivets in it) adds a glorious texture to the lush harmonies, sparse but solid, allowing the strings to ring. Bill begins the track with a single note that seems to fill the entire room. Playing with *feeling* was always the most important aspect of Bill Evans music, and it is here in abundance.

The poignancy of this film about a wartime romance is brought to life by Bill, Scott, and Paul on the recording *Waltz for Debby,* but a lot of serious thought and effort went into this seemingly spare and spontaneous performance live from the Village Vanguard on June 25, 1961.

"That's the thing that everybody seems to miss," Bill told *DownBeat* in 1964. "By giving ourselves a solid base on which to work ... then we can make any shapes we want, any lines we want ... And if we have the skill, we can just about do anything. Then we are really free."[17]

However, not everyone was aware of or appreciative of the effort Bill put into his music to make it sound so personal. Because Bill possessed such a comprehensive knowledge of jazz and jazz styles as well as classical literature, he was often labeled an "intellectual" player. Even fans like New Yorker jazz critic Whitney Balliett wrote "no musician relies less on intuition than Bill Evans."[18] Here is what Bill said on this particular subject during one of the best interviews he ever did on air with CBC Radio Host Ted O'Reilly in May, 1980: "I think that intuition has to lead [your] knowledge, but it can't be out there on its own, you know? If it's on its own, you're going to flounder sooner or later."[19]

What this says to me is that your intuition makes the split-second decisions of what to play after instantly accessing whatever knowledge you have. This is a miraculous process that jazz musicians have been doing since the beginning of the music.

***

A Carnegie Hall Experience
March 29, 1980

Over the years, I've been fortunate to have performed at Carnegie Hall many times with artists such as Chuck Mangione, Tony Bennett, and the Count Basie Orchestra. While these were all incredible events, the most memorable was a concert with the Bill Evans Trio for the Newport Jazz Festival in 1979. The music was, of course, outstanding, as always whenever Bill performed. But what made this concert so memorable were the events leading up to it.

The concert, produced by George Wein, was a double bill featuring Bill's trio and singer Sarah Vaughan with her own trio. Mel Tormé served as Master of Ceremonies. After the usual sound check, we all broke for dinner. Bassist Marc Johnson and I found a place nearby and were back in the hall by around 7:00 p.m. Bill had decided to drive back to his apartment in Fort Lee but had plenty of time to return for this show even at rush hour.

By 7:15 p.m., however, heads were being counted backstage and all were present except Bill. By 7:30 p.m., all eyes were on Bill's manager, Helen Keane, who had been frantically trying to locate Bill. Keep in mind that these were pre-cell phone days. Mel Tormé was visibly upset, and the agent from George Wein's office also seemed concerned. We all were, quite frankly, because Bill was always punctual, a total professional.

Finally, at 7:45 p.m., Bill arrived at the stage door and all movement stopped dead because he had a bandage across his nose, his glasses held together with another Band-Aid, stitches on his brow, his left arm in a sling and encased in a cast up to the knuckles! Everyone was speechless except Bill who casually asked, "What time is it?" The shocked response from someone was, "It's a quarter to 8," to which Bill replied, "Great, I have time for a cup of coffee." He then proceeded to find one and enjoy it before standing by in the wings for the call to go on stage.

When the trio was announced, we walked onstage and there was a collective gasp from the packed house. Without any further announcement, Bill took his seat at the piano, removed his left arm from the sling and placed it on the keyboard. From that moment on, it was as if nothing whatsoever was physically wrong with him. From my perspective at the drums, all I ever saw was Bill's head and occasionally his right arm rose into view—usually to push his glasses back up on his nose—but by all appearances and from what I was hearing, nothing was out of the ordinary. The music was flowing and inspired, and the audience response reflected this.

Tony Bennett used to say to me: "Never follow a sailor on crutches at an amateur show" and that was pretty much the same on this evening. Bill broke it up.

Later, he told us what happened. While driving home on the West Side Highway, it started raining and his windshield wipers failed. As a result of poor vision, he hit a massive pothole and then slammed into the center divider. At the emergency room the attending physician wanted to put the cast on all the way up to his fingertips but Bill said, *No, I have a gig tonight, so stop at the knuckles!*

Not one engagement was cancelled as a result of this accident and this same scene was repeated over and over for weeks while we fulfilled our contracts at various concert halls and night clubs. No one was disappointed by our performance during this period.

For the remainder of his life, I witnessed Bill Evans overcome the frailties of his physical being many times with an indomitable spirit. He would say that *My exterior may be a wreck but inside I'm pure.* It must have been true.

Itinerary

Compiled by Tonino Vantaggiato

January 17–20, 1979, Bijou Café, Philadelphia, PA

January 23–27, 1979, Rick's Café Americain, Chicago, IL

January 29, 1979, Northrop Auditorium, University of Minnesota, Minneapolis, MN

January 30, 1979, The Maintenance Shop, Iowa State University, Ames, IA

February 2, 1979, Paradiso, Santa Cruz, CA

February 3–4, 1979, Great American Music Hall, San Francisco, CA

February 13–18, 1979, Village Vanguard, New York City, NY

February 20–25, 1979, Rising Sun Celebrity Jazz Club, Montreal, Quebec, Canada

February 26–27, 1979, Jonathan Swift's, Cambridge, MA

April 12, 1979, Ridge Theatre, Vancouver, Canada

April 13–14, 1979, Mayflower Restaurant, Edmonton, Canada

April 15, 1979, The Calgary Inn, Calgary, Canada (Note: The trio never performed. Bill refused to play after the promoter supplied a damaged piano and refused to repair it by showtime.)

April 17–22, 1979, Blues Alley, Washington, D.C. (Note: Bill performed the first three nights and abruptly stopped playing as the gig started on April 20 after learning of his brother Harry's death. Pianist Marc Copland [then Cohen] played the remaining nights with a local rhythm section.)

April 26–May 2, 1979 (dates are estimate), Weeklong series of clinics at the following venues: University of Arizona, Prima Community College, Amphitheatre High School, Canyon Del Oro High School, Sunnyside High School, Cross Junior High School and several community centers. Tucson, AZ

April 28, 1979, The Temple of Music and Art, Tucson, AZ

May 1, 1979, El Pueblo Neighborhood Center, Tucson, AZ

May 5, 1979, Berklee Performance Center, Berklee College of Music, Boston, MA

May 11–12, 1979, The Bottom Line, New York City, NY

June 3, 1979, Symphony Space, New York City, NY

June 19–24, 1979, Village Vanguard, New York City, NY

July 3–8, 1979, Basin Street Club, Toronto, Ontario, Canada

July 9, 1979. Hartford Festival of Jazz, Bushnell Park, Hartford, CT

July 11–14, 1979, Bijou Café, Philadelphia, PA

July 24–28, 1979 and July 31–August 4, 1979, Rick's Café Americain, Chicago, IL

September 4–9, 11–16, 1979, Village Vanguard, New York City, NY

September 19, 1979, Teatro Opera, Buenos Aires, Argentina

September 24, 1979, Teatro El Círculo, Rosario, Argentina

September 25, 1979, Teatro Municipal, San Nicolas, Argentina

September 27, 1979, Teatro General Municipal San Martin, Buenos Aires, Argentina

September 29, 1979 and October 1, 1979, Sala Cecília Meireles, Rio De Janeiro, Brazil (Note: Following the September 29 concert, Bill sat in at Chiko's Bar, the home of pianist-composer Luiz Eça, performing solo, duos with Marc Johnson, and four-hand duets with Eça. Joe did not play as there was no drum set available.)

October 6 and 7, 1979, Meany Hall for the Performing Arts, University of Washington, Seattle, WA

October 9, 1979, Great American Music Hall, San Francisco, CA

October 19, 1979, Hancher Auditorium, Iowa City, IA

October 30 to November 3, Lulu White's, Boston, MA

November 4, 1979, Symphony Hall, Memorial Arts Center, Atlanta, GA

November 6, 1979, Southeastern Louisiana University, Hammond, LA

November 7, 1979, University of North Texas, Lyceum Theater, Denton, TX

November 16, 1979, Théâtre Femina, Bordeaux, France

November 17, 1979, Muziekzentrum Vredenburg, Utrecht, The Netherlands

November 21, 1979, Jazzhus Montmartre, Copenhagen, Denmark

November 24, 1979, Teatro Morlacchi, Perugia, Italy

November 26, 1979, Espace Cardin, Paris, France

November 28, 1979, Estudios TVE, Esplugues De Llobregat, Spain

November 29, 1979, New Morning, Geneva, Switzerland

November 30, 1979, Teatro Politeama, Casale Monferrato, Italy

December 1, 1979, Municipal Theater "Francesco Cilea," Reggio Calabria, Italy

December 2, 1979, Teatro Biondo, Palermo, Italy

December 3, 1979, Liederhalle, Stuttgart, Germany

December 4, 1979, Auditorium Maurice Ravel, Lyon, France

December 5, 1979, Jazz Club (Hans Rossbach), Koblenz, Germany

December 6, 1979, De Meerkoet, Lelystad, The Netherlands

December 8, 1979, Grote Zaal de Oosterpoort, Groningen, The Netherlands

December 10, 1979, Music Inn, Rome, Italy

December 11–12, 1979, Balboa Jazz Club, Madrid, Spain

December 13, 1979, Teatre Principal de València, Valencia, Spain

January 8–13, 1980, Rising Sun Celebrity Jazz Club, Montreal, Canada

January 15–20, 1980, Village Vanguard, New York City, NY

March 9, 1980, Berklee Performance Center, Berklee College of Music, Boston, MA

March 15, 1980, Proctors Theatre, Schenectady, NY

March 29, 1980, Carnegie Hall, New York City, NY

April 2–6, 1980, Lulu White's, Boston, MA

April 27, 1980, Sanders Theatre, Harvard University, Cambridge, MA

May 3, 1980, Cornell College, King Memorial Chapel, Mt. Vernon, IA

May 4, 1980, Bach Dancing & Dynamite Society, Half Moon Bay, CA

May 9, 1980, Zellerbach Hall, University of California, Berkeley, CA

May 13–17 and 20–24, 1980, Rick's Café Americain, Chicago, IL

May 27 to June 1, 1980 and June 3–8, 1980, Village Vanguard, New York City, NY

June 13–14, 1980, The Office Jazz Club, Nyack, NY

July 7–12, 1980, Basin Street Club, Toronto, Canada

July 14, 1980, Zeleste, Barcelona, Spain

July 17, 1980, Castel Sant'Angelo, Rome, Italy

July 18, 1980, Castello Sforzesco (Sforza Castle), Milan, Italy

July 19, 1980, Chiostro Di Santa Chiara, Brescia, Italy

July 20, 1980, Théâtre de Verdure, La Grande Motte, France

July 21 to August 2, 1980, Ronnie Scott's Jazz Club, London, England

August 3, 1980, Gouvy Jazz & Blues Festival, Gouvy, Belgium

August 5, 1980, Jazzhus Montmartre, Copenhagen, Denmark (Note: Bill was ill, so Joe and Marc performed with Bob Rockwell on tenor. See Chapter 17.)

August 7, 1980, Molde International Jazz Festival, Molde, Norway

August 9, 1980, Piazzale Terme, Santa Cesarea Terme, Italy

August 10, 1980, Piazzale Lenio Flacco, Brindisi, Italy (Note: This concert ended abruptly after Bill complained about someone blaring a radio from an apartment window over the piazza. Bill asked the promoter to get it turned off. But the promoter was reluctant to do it. So Bill ended the concert after just a few tunes.)

August 11, 1980, Villa Comunale, San Severo, Italy

August 12, 1980, Cineteatro Valentino, Castellaneta, Italy

August 13, 1980, Sala Dei Templari, Art Museum, Molfetta, Italy

August 15, 1980, Private Party, Home of Fritz Feltens, Bad Hönningen, West Germany

August 21, 1980, Northwest Service Center, Portland, OR

August 23, 1980, Merv Griffin Show (taping for later broadcast), Los Angeles, CA (Note: Bill accompanied by Ray Brown, bass; and Nick Ceroli, drums.)

August 27, 1980, Hollywood Bowl, Los Angeles, CA

August 31 to September 8, 1980, Keystone Korner, San Francisco, CA

September 9–14, 1980, Fat Tuesday's, New York City, NY (Note: Bill Evans played the first two nights but could not complete the booking due to illness. Pianist Andy LaVerne performed with Marc and Joe for the duration of the engagement.)

Bill Evans Trio Recordings

Unless otherwise noted, personnel for all recordings are Bill Evans, piano; Marc Johnson, bass; and Joe La Barbera, drums.

1. **Bill Evans Trio Live At The Maintenance Shop '79** Video, (Vap (J) VPVR 60647). Television broadcast, The Maintenance Shop, Ames, Iowa. January 30, 1979. The performances that produced this video are described in detail in Chapter 5.

2. **Bill Evans—Last Performance** Video, (Victor Entertainment (J) VIVJ 1). Second set of Ames, Iowa concert. Second set of preceding Ames, Iowa show. See Chapter 5.

3. **Bill Evans—We Will Meet Again** (Warner Bros. HS 3411-Y). Tom Harrell, trumpet 1–3, 5, 6, 8; Larry Schneider, tenor, soprano sax 1–3, 5, 6, 8; Bill Evans, piano, electric piano; Marc Johnson, bass 1–3, 5, 6, 8; Joe La Barbera, drums 1–3, 5, 6, 8. August 6–9, 1979. Recorded at CBS 30th Street Studio, New York City, N.Y. Truly a highlight for Marc, Tom, Larry and me to record in this legendary recording studio. Details in Chapter 7.

4. **Bill Evans Trio—Live In Buenos Aires 1979** (Yellow Note (Argentine) Y-200). Teatro Municipal General San Martin, Buenos Aires, Argentina, September 27, 1979. This concert was memorable because the audience was so enthusiastic and warm. The night before we heard bandoneon master Walter Rios perform at Caño Night Club. See Chapter 9.

5. **Bill Evans—Homecoming (Live At Southeastern Louisiana University, 1979)** (Milestone MCD-9291-2). Southeastern Louisiana University, Hammond, La., November 6, 1979. Bill was very pleased to perform at his alma mater with the trio. It was also on this night that a bullet narrowly missed hitting one of us at dinner. See Chapter 21.

6. **Bill Evans—The Paris Concert, Edition 1** (Elektra Musician E1-60164). L'Espace Cardin, Paris, France, November 26, 1979. These two live recordings are discussed in detail in Chapter 13.

7. **Bill Evans—The Paris Concert, Edition 2** (Elektra Musician E1-60311). Same as previous session. See Chapter 13.

8. **Bill Evans Trio—Live at Balboa Jazz Club, Vol. 1** (Ivory (Portuguese) ILP-3000). Balboa Jazz Club, Madrid, Spain. December 12, 1979. The audience in Spain was as enthusiastic as those in Buenos Aires. Bill was very well received during our stay in Madrid.

9. **Bill Evans Trio—Live at Balboa Jazz Club, Vol. 2** (Ivory (Portuguese) ILP-3001). Same session.

10. **Bill Evans Trio—Live at Balboa Jazz Club, Vol. 3** (Ivory (Portuguese) ILP-3002). Same session.

11. **Bill Evans Trio—Live at Balboa Jazz Club, Vol. 4** (Ivory (Portuguese) ILP-3003). Balboa Jazz Club, Madrid, Spain, December 11, 1979.

12. **Bill Evans Trio—Live at Balboa Jazz Club, Vol. 5** (Ivory (Portuguese) ILP-3004). Same as previous session.

13. **The Brilliant Bill Evans** (West Wind (G) WW 2058). Rome, Italy, 1979. I have a few photos from the night we performed outdoors on a warm evening to a receptive crowd in Rome. Marc sounds amazing on this recording!

14. **Bill Evans—Turn Out the Stars: The Final Village Vanguard Sessions-June 1980** (Warner Bros. 45925). Village Vanguard, New York City, N.Y., June 4–6 and 8, 1980. These sessions took place over four nights at the Vanguard and required a lot of preparation. A new piano had to be delivered and recording engineer Malcolm Addey had to take over a large portion of the kitchen for his console. I was so embarrassed by the number of microphones on the drums, which gave the appearance of me being the feature of the performance, but, of course, the recording was excellent.

15. **Bill Evans—Letter To Evan** (Dreyfus Jazz (F) 191064-2). Ronnie Scott's Jazz Club, London, England, July 21, 1980. I always looked forward to playing at Ronnie Scott's in London. The trio was sounding very good, but Bill's health was seriously deteriorating. I think the person who recorded this was an acquaintance of Bill's.

16. **Bill Evans—Turn Out the Stars** (Dreyfus Jazz (F) 191063-2). Ronnie Scott's Jazz Club, London, England, August 2, 1980.

17. **Bill Evans—His Last Live In Germany** (West Wind (G) WW 2022). Bad Hönningen, West Germany, August 15, 1980. This concert was

fraught from the start. We arrived in the afternoon on time, but suddenly Bill demanded he be driven back to the hotel which took a couple of hours. More details in Chapter 17.

18. **Bill Evans Trio—The Last Waltz** (Milestone 8MCD-4430-2). Keystone Korner, San Francisco, Calif., August 31–September 8, 1980. The recordings made during our extended stay at this club have been issued several times. Bill was very weak by now, spending most of the day in bed. But once he hit the stage, he played beautifully as always. See Chapter 18.

19. **The Bill Evans Trio—Consecration** (Milestone 8MCD-4436-2). Same as previous session. Keystone Korner, August 31–September 8, 1980.

20. **Bill Evans Trio—Live at Casale Monferrato** (Codec Records 441). Piedmont, Italy, November 30, 1979. If I remember correctly, this was outdoors in the warm evening of Piedmont. Italian audiences loved Bill, and he gave them what they came for. The quality of this recording is so poor. It sounds as though someone put a cassette recorder in front of a PA monitor.

21. **Bill Evans Trio—Concert at Rising Sun** (All Blues Records ABR-033). Montreal, Canada, January 1980. Another good gig and sold out, nightly as I recall. The biggest issue is that the stage was not carpeted which created a distracting low-end rumble.. Bill's foot beating time is a distraction, but the music is very good.

22. **Bill Evans—The Sesjun Radio Shows** (Out Of The Blue (Du) PRCD2011005). Taken from live radio broadcasts in the Netherlands. Bill Evans, piano; Eddie Gomez, bass. De Boerenhofstede, Laren, the Netherlands, December 13, 1973. Bill Evans, piano; Eddie Gomez, bass; Eliot Zigmund, drums; De Boerenhofstede, Laren, the Netherlands, February 13, 1975. Bill Evans, piano; Marc Johnson, bass; Joe La Barbera, drums; with Toots Thielemans, harmonica 5–9, De Meerkoet, Lelystad, the Netherlands, December 6, 1979. This was a reunion for me with Toots, who I played with when I auditioned for Bill. Bill and Marc had already recorded with Toots, who jokingly referred to his harmonica as a "chrome sandwich!"

23. **Bill Evans Trio**—Molde, Norway. Video, Molde International Jazz Festival, August 7, 1980. Available on youtube.com https://www. youtube.com/watch?v=ZeSQi489xfg We were exhausted by the time we arrived here, and we had to depart immediately after the performance. I think everyone in the hall realized what was happening. Bill looked awful but somehow mustered the strength to give an outstanding concert. The version of "Your Story" at this show is so compelling.

24. **Jazz Entre Amigos**—Barcelona, Spain, 1980. Video available on youtube.com   https://www.youtube.com/watch?v=cLWttdHVj80&feature=emb_logo, This was shot during our first stop in Spain. The video is interspersed with commentary from a presenter.

25. **Bill Evans Trio**—Rome, Italy, Live at the Music Inn, December 10, 1979. This concert is available on numerous youtube.com links. Here's one: https://www.youtube.com/watch?v=hk1aHSdeWe0. This venue was positively claustrophobic, more like a cave than a nightclub. There was only one way in and one way out. I remember that by the time we arrived, the spill-over crowd completely blocked the entrance and our local road manager had to lift Marc's bass in the air over his head as we forged our way inside.

26. **Bill Evans Time Remembered.** 2015, Produced by Bruce Spiegel, who did an incredible job creating this documentary about Bill's life. He painstakingly tracked down and interviewed people everywhere who are pertinent to the story. There is much footage that I had never seen before, including scenes with Peri Cousins (of "Peri's Scope" fame), who I came to know after moving to Los Angeles.

Endnotes

Notes for Chapter 1

1. *Big Wave Hits Ship, Four Perish By It,* New York Times, November 11, 1911.
2. *Jazz Track,* Miles Davis CD, Release date, November 1959, Tracks, https://en.wikipedia.org/wiki/Jazz_Track; https://www.discogs.com/Miles-Davis-Jazz-Track/release/511939.

Notes for Chapter 2

1. Simon Rios, *Fred Taylor, Who Spent His Life Supporting the Boston Jazz Scene, Dies at 90,* WBUR-FM, October 26, 2019, https://www.wbur.org/artery/2019/10/26/fred-taylor-boston-jazz-scene.
2. *Lenox History,* Lenox School of Jazz, February 11, 2016, https://lenoxhistory.org/lenoxhistorypeopleandplaces/music-inn-lenox-school-jazz/.

Notes for Chapter 3

1. Mob ownership of The Sands, https://en.wikipedia.org/wiki/Sands_Hotel_and_Casino.
2. Mike Weatherford, *Frank Sinatra,* Las Vegas Review Journal, February 7, 1999, https://www.reviewjournal.com/news/frank-sinatra/.
3. Peter Erskine, *No Beethoven,* Reprinted by permission of author, (Santa Monica: Fuzzy Music, 2013), 49–50.
4. Peter Erskine, Interview by email, October 11, 2020.
5. Alphonso Johnson, Interview by email, February 4, 2021.
6. Bill Minor, *Monterey Jazz Festival, Forty Legendary Years*, (Santa Monica: Angel City Press, 1997), 162.
7. Michelle Norris, *Billy Crystal: My Uncle Milt,* NPR, August 15, 2005, https://www.npr.org/templates/story/story.php?storyId=4601031; Jim Bickal, *For Comedian Billy Crystal, All That (Dixieland) Jazz Is All in the Family,* Minnesota Public Radio, October 16, 2013, https://www.mprnews.org/story/2013/10/16/for-comedian-billy-crystal-all-that-dixieland-jazz-is-all-in-the-family.

Notes for Chapter 4

1. Bill Evans discography, allmusic.com, https://www.allmusic.com/artist/bill-evans-mn0000764702/discography.

2. Evans Grammy wins by 1979, https://www.grammy.com/grammys/artists/bill-evans/9689.
3. Marc Johnson, Interview by author, March 26, 2016.
4. Faye Anderson, All That Philly Jazz, *Douglass Hotel*, April 7, 2015, https://phillyjazz.us/2015/04/07/douglass-hotel/.
5. John Di Martino, Interview by author, February 17, 2016.

Notes for Chapter 5

1. Marc Johnson, Interview by author, March 26, 2016.
2. Gary Novak, Interview by email, January 29, 2021.
3. Maintenance Shop, Iowa State University, History, Club Size, https://www.discogs.com/label/1832695-The-Maintenance-Shop. https://www.sub.iastate.edu/maintenance-shop/history-of-the-venue/.
4. Tonya Weber, Iowa Public Television. Email to confirm broadcast dates of Maintenance Shop Concert, May 27, 2016.
5. *'58 Miles*, Release date, 1974, https://en.wikipedia.org/wiki/1958_Miles https://www.allmusic.com/album/58-sessions-featuring-stella-by-starlight-mw0000194393.
6. Carole Shifrin, Airline Machinists Strike, *Machinists Strike Against United Airlines*, Washington Post, March 31, 1979, https://www.washingtonpost.com/archive/politics/1979/03/31/machinists-strike-united-airlines/610c2eef-9f11-455d-912d-d3364d1ae08f/.
7. Laurie Verchomin, Interview by email, September 10, 2016.
8. Malcolm Page, Calgary concert, Interview by author, November 9, 2014.
9. Tunde Agbi, Calgary concert, Interview by author, September 10, 2016.
10. Marc Johnson, Blues Alley gig, Interview by author, April 18, 2016.
11. Marc Copland, Blues Alley gig, Interview by email, August 26, 2016.

Notes for Chapter 6

1. Ross Porter, Canadian Broadcasting Corporation, Radio Interview, *Bill Evans home and car interview by Ross Porter on JAZZFM91,* YouTube, https://www.youtube.com/watch?v=L1Sz5ZNokEA.
2. Andy LaVerne, Getting a piano lesson with Bill, Interview by author, April 23, 2019.

Notes for Chapter 7

1. Steve Hoffman, *History of CBS Records 30th Street Studio NYC,* https://forums.stevehoffman.tv/threads/history-of-cbs-records-30th-street-studio-nyc-many-pictures.388186/, Wikipedia, CBS 30th Street Studio, https://en.wikipedia.org/wiki/CBS_30th_Street_Studio.

2. Robin D.G. Kelley, CBS 30th Street Studio, *Thelonious Monk: The Life and Times of an American Original*, (New York: Free Press, 2009), 327.

3. Frank Laico, Engineering Credits, https://www.allmusic.com/artist/frank-laico-mn0000142372/credits.

4. Marc Johnson, Recording *We Will Meet Again*, Interview by email, November 10, 2016.

5. *We Will Meet Again*, Grammy Awards, https://www.grammy.com/grammys/awards/23rd-annual-grammy-awards-1980.

6. *We Will Meet Again*, allmusic.com rating, https://www.allmusic.com/album/we-will-meet-again-mw0000276230.

Notes for Chapter 8

1. Bill Evans, Letter to the Editor on Russia, DownBeat, *Chords & Discords,* October, 1980.

Notes for Chapter 9

1. Manhattan Plaza, https://www.related.com/our-company/properties/manhattan-plaza; https://en.wikipedia.org/wiki/Manhattan_Plaza; Joseph Fried, *Manhattan Plaza Wins Approval As Housing for Performing Artists*, New York Times, February 4, 1977, https://www.nytimes.com/1977/02/04/archives/manhattan-plaza-wins-approval-as-housing-for-performing-artists.html.

2. Garry Dial, Interviews by author, November 2, 2014; December 2, 2016.

Notes for Chapter 10

1. Ross Porter, Canadian Broadcasting Corporation, *Bill Evans home and car interview by Ross Porter on JAZZFM91,* YouTube, https://www.youtube.com/watch?v=L1Sz5ZNokEA.

2. Dick Buckley, Bill Evans interview, WBEZ Radio, Chicago, August 1, 1979. Cassette courtesy of Joe La Barbera.

3. Georgia Urban, *Bill Evans off The Keyboard,* The Entertainer, Schenectady, NY, March 14, 1980.

4. Ross Porter, Canadian Broadcasting Corporation, *Bill Evans home and car interview by Ross Porter on JAZZFM91,* YouTube, https://www.youtube.com/watch?v=L1Sz5ZNokEA.

5. Georgia Urban, *Bill Evans off The Keyboard,* The Entertainer, Schenectady, NY, March 14, 1980.

Notes for Chapter 11

1. Helen Keane, Peggy Kenas, Executive Producers, *The Universal Mind of Bill Evans: The Creative Process and Self Teaching*, https://www.youtube.com/watch?v=QwXAqIaUahI.
2. The Rockefeller University, *The First Pharmacological Treatment for Narcotic Addiction: Methadone Maintenance*, http://centennial.rucares.org/index.php?page=Methadone_Maintenance.

Notes for Chapter 13

1. L'Espace Cardin, History, Seating, https://fr.wikipedia.org/wiki/Espace_Cardin.
2. Ben Ratliff, *Francis Paudras, 62, Patron of Jazz Pianist Bud Powell*, New York Times, December 17, 1997, https://www.nytimes.com/1997/12/17/arts/francis-paudras-62-patron-of-jazz-pianist-bud-powell.html.

Notes for Chapter 14

1. James Covert, *The Syms Saga: From Rags to Riches*, New York Post, November 3, 2011, https://nypost.com/2011/11/03/the-syms-saga-from-rags-to-riches-to-rags/.
2. Gene Lees, *Meet Me at Jim and Andy's: Jazz Musicians and Their World*, (New York: Oxford University Press, 1988), 162–163.
3. Sondra Gair, Interview with Bill Evans, WBEZ, November 14, 1976. Digital copy courtesy of Joe La Barbera.

Notes for Chapter 15

1. allmusic.com, Live at the Village Vanguard titles, https://www.allmusic.com/search/all/live%20at%20the%20village%20vanguard.
2. Peter Watrous, *Max Gordon, 86, Jazz Promoter and Founder of Vanguard, Dies*, New York Times, May 12, 1989, https://www.nytimes.com/1989/05/12/obituaries/max-gordon-86-jazz-promoter-and-founder-of-vanguard-dies.html.
3. Scott Yanow, *Turn Out the Stars* Album review, allmusic.com, https://www.allmusic.com/album/turn-out-the-stars-final-village-vanguard-recordings-mw0000080506.
4. Michael Bloom, Bill Evans' Last Interview, Klacto, Hawaii's Jazz Magazine, October 1980, courtesy of Joe La Barbera.
5. Dick Buckley, Bill Evans interview, WBEZ Radio, Chicago, August 1, 1979. Cassette courtesy of Joe La Barbera.
6. Tiffany La Barbera-Palmer, Interview by author, July 15, 2018.

Notes for Chapter 17

1. Jim Aikin, *The Essence of Jazz Piano,* Contemporary Keyboard Magazine, June 1980.
2. Ronnie Scott's, *History and Acts*, Ronnie Scott's, https://www.ronniescotts. co.uk/about-ronnies/club-history.
3. David Fricke, *Charlie Watts' Jazz Dream*, Rolling Stone, February 26, 1987, https://www.rollingstone.com/music/music-news/charlie-watts-jazz-dream-249051/.
4. Marc Johnson, Interview by email, March 28, 2019.

Notes for Chapter 18

1. Merv Griffin Show, August 23, 1980 (Taping), September 23, 1980 (Air date), Video courtesy of Joe La Barbera.
2. Denny Zeitlin, Playing at Keystone Korner before Bill arrived, Interview by author, May 13, 2019.
3. Richie Beirach, Hearing Bill's last gig at Fat Tuesday's, Interview by email, January 5, 2021.
4. Adam Nussbaum, Hearing Bill's last gig at Fat Tuesday's, Interview by email, January 8, 2021.
5. Andy LaVerne, Subbing for Bill's final nights at Fat Tuesday's, Interview by author, April 23, 2019.
6. Andy LaVerne, Joe and Marc initially not getting paid at Fat Tuesday's, Interview by email, April 24, 2019.

Notes for Chapter 19

1. Jon Mayer, Interview by author, January 25, 2015.

Notes for Chapter 21

1. Ian Carr, *Miles Davis: The Definitive Biography* (London: Paladin Books, Granada Publishing 1984), 68.
2. Rod Starns, Interview with Bill Evans, *Homecoming* (Live concert CD), Milestone 1979.
3. Terry Teachout, *Suicide Was Painful*, New York Times, September 13, 1998, https://www.nytimes.com/1998/09/13/books/suicide-was-painful.html.
4. Jan Stevens, Interview with Nenette Evans, The Bill Evans Webpages, https://www.billevanswebpages.com/nenette.html.
5. George Klabin, Interview with Bill Evans, *Pieces of Jade*, Resonance Records, 2009.

Notes for Appendix

1. Svein Erik Borja, Producer, NRK, *Bill Evans' Post-Concert Interview at the Molde, Norway Jazz Festival*, https://www.youtube.com/watch?v=UmvxPLFuHaM, (c. August 7, 1980).
2. Jim Franksen, *Jazz Record Reviews,* Jazz and Pop, October 1967.
3. Balleras (No first name in byline), *Record Reviews*, DownBeat, Review of *The Tokyo Concert*, December 1974.
4. Martin Williams, *The Jazz Hit of Montreux*, New York Times, January 5, 1969, https://www.nytimes.com/1969/01/05/archives/the-jazz-hit-of montreux.html.
5. Michael Bourne, *Bill Evans,* Radio Free Jazz, October 1976.
6. Robert Kenselaar, *Breakfast with Bill Evans*, The Aquarian, May 9–16, 1979.
7. Robert Palmer, *Bill Evans: Chemistry and the Piano Trio*, Rolling Stone, October 4, 1979.
8. François Lacharme, *Sorrow in Soho*, *Jazz Magazine* (France), October 2010, Reprinted in full with permission of the author.
9. Martin Williams, *Introducing Scott LaFaro,* DownBeat, August 1960.
10. John Mehegan, *Bill Evans: An Interview by John Mehegan*, Jazz Magazine, date unknown. Photocopy, courtesy of Joe La Barbera.
11. Nat Hentoff, *Introducing Bill Evans,* DownBeat, October 1959.
12. Don Nelson, *Bill Evans,* Interview with Bill, DownBeat, December 1960.
13. Gene Lees, *Inside The New Bill Evans Trio*, DownBeat, November 22, 1962.
14. Gene Lees, *Re: Person I Knew,* The Gene Lees JazzLetter, 1984. Photocopy, courtesy of Joe La Barbera.
15. Ross Porter, Canadian Broadcasting Corporation, *Bill Evans home and car interview by Ross Porter on JAZZFM91,* YouTube, https://www.youtube.com/watch?v=L1Sz5ZNokEA.
16. Scott LaFaro, *My Foolish Heart*, Rehearsal Recording, *Pieces of Jade*, Resonance Records, 2009.
17. Dan Morgenstern, *The Art of Playing*, DownBeat, October 22, 1964.
18. Gene Lees, Whitney Balliett's quote, originally from a New Yorker story, *Bill Evans—The Pianist and The Man*, International Musician, c. 1964. Photocopy, courtesy of Joe La Barbera.
19. Ted O'Reilly, Interview with Bill Evans, Canadian Broadcasting Corporation, May 1980, Digital copy, courtesy of Joe La Barbera.

Bibliography

Books

Carr, Ian. *Miles Davis: The Definitive Biography*, (London: Paladin Books, Granada Publishing 1984).

Erskine, Peter. *No Beethoven*, Reprinted by permission of author, (Santa Monica: Fuzzy Music, 2013).

Kelley, Robin D.G. *Thelonious Monk: The Life and Times of an American Original*, (New York: Free Press, 2009).

Lees, Gene. *Meet Me at Jim and Andy's: Jazz Musicians and Their World*, (New York: Oxford University Press, 1988).

Minor, Bill. *Monterey Jazz Festival, Forty Legendary Years*, (Santa Monica: Angel City Press, 1997).

Verchomin, Laurie. *The Big Love, Life and Death With Bill Evans*, (Self-published, 2010).

Newspapers, Magazines, Newsletters

Big Wave Hits Ship, Four Perish By It, New York Times, November 11, 1911.

Aikin, Jim. *The Essence of Jazz Piano*, Contemporary Keyboard Magazine, June 1980.

Balleras (No first name in byline), *Record Reviews*, DownBeat, Review of *The Tokyo Concert*, December 1974.

Bloom, Michael. *Bill Evans' Last Interview*, Klacto, Hawaii's Jazz Magazine, October 1980. Courtesy of Joe La Barbera.

Bourne, Michael. *Bill Evans*, Radio Free Jazz, October 1976.

Covert, James. *The Syms Saga: From Rags to Riches*, New York Post, November 3, 2011, https://nypost.com/2011/11/03/the-syms-saga-from-rags-to-riches-to-rags/.

Evans, Bill. Letter to the Editor on Russia, DownBeat, *Chords & Discords*, October, 1980.

Franksen, Jim. *Jazz Record Reviews*, Jazz and Pop, October 1967.

Fricke, David. *Charlie Watts' Jazz Dream*, Rolling Stone, February 26, 1987, https://www.rollingstone.com/music/music-news/charlie-watts-jazz-dream-249051/.

Fried, Joseph. *Manhattan Plaza Wins Approval as Housing for Performing Artists*, New York Times, February 4, 1977, https://www.nytimes.com/1977/02/04/archives/manhattan-plaza-wins-approval-as-housing-for-performing-artists.html.

Hentoff, Nat. *Introducing Bill Evans,* DownBeat, October 1959.

Kenselaar, Robert. *Breakfast with Bill Evans*, The Aquarian, May 9–16, 1979.

Lacharme, François. *Sorrow in Soho*, *Jazz Magazine* (France), October 2010, reprinted in full with permission of the author.

Lees, Gene. *Inside The New Bill Evans Trio*, DownBeat, November 22, 1962.

Lees, Gene. *Re: Person I Knew,* The Gene Lees JazzLetter, 1984. Photocopy, courtesy of Joe La Barbera.

Lees, Gene. Whitney Balliett quote, *Bill Evans—The Pianist and The Man,* International Musician, c. 1964. Photocopy, courtesy of Joe La Barbera.

Mehegan, John. *Bill Evans: An Interview by John Mehegan*, Jazz Magazine, date unknown. Photocopy, courtesy of Joe La Barbera.

Morgenstern, Dan. *The Art of Playing*, DownBeat, October 22, 1964.

Nelson, Don. *Bill Evans,* Interview with Bill, DownBeat, December 1960.

Palmer, Robert. *Bill Evans: Chemistry and the Piano Trio,* Rolling Stone, October 4, 1979.

Ratliff, Ben. *Francis Paudras, 62, Patron of Jazz Pianist Bud Powell*, New York Times, December 17, 1997, https://www.nytimes.com/1997/12/17/arts/francis-paudras-62-patron-of-jazz-pianist-bud-powell.html.

Shifrin, Carole. *Machinists Strike Against United Airlines*, Washington Post, March 31, 1979, https://www.washingtonpost.com/archive/politics/1979/03/31/machinists-strike-united-airlines/610c2eef-9f11-455d-912d-d3364d1ae08f/.

Teachout, Terry. *Suicide Was Painful*, New York Times, September 13, 1998, https://www.nytimes.com/1998/09/13/books/suicide-was-painful.html.

Urban, Georgia. *Bill Evans off The Keyboard,* The Entertainer, Schenectady, NY, March 14, 1980.

Watrous, Peter. *Max Gordon, 86, Jazz Promoter And Founder of Vanguard, Dies*, New York Times, May 12, 1989, https://www.nytimes.com/1989/05/12/obituaries/max-gordon-86-jazz-promoter-and-founder-of-vanguard-dies.html.

Weatherford, Mike. *Frank Sinatra,* Las Vegas Review Journal, February 7, 1999, https://www.reviewjournal.com/news/frank-sinatra/.

Williams, Martin. *The Jazz Hit of Montreux*, New York Times, January 5, 1969, https://www.nytimes.com/1969/01/05/archives/the-jazz-hit-of-montreux.html.

Williams, Martin. *Introducing Scott LaFaro,* DownBeat, August 1960.

Interviews by Authors

Agbi, Tunde. Interview by author, September 10, 2016.

Beirach, Richie. Interview by email, January 5, 2021.

Copland, Marc. Interview by email, August 26, 2016.

Dial, Garry. Interviews by author, November 2, 2014; December 2, 2016.

Di Martino, John. Interview by author, February 17, 2016.

Erskine, Peter. Interview by email, October 11, 2020.

Johnson, Alphonso. Interview by email, February 4, 2021.

Johnson, Marc. Interviews by author, March 26, 2016; April 18, 2016; July 27, 2016; November 10, 2016; March 28, 2019.

La Barbera-Palmer, Tiffany. Interview by author, July 15, 2018.

LaVerne, Andy. Interview by author, April 23, 2019; April 24, 2019.

Mayer, Jon. Interview by author, January 25, 2015.

Novak, Gary. Interview by email, January 29, 2021.

Nussbaum, Adam. Interview by email, January 8, 2021.

Page, Malcolm. Interview by author, November 9, 2014.

Verchomin, Laurie. Interview by email, September 10, 2016.

Weber, Tonya. Iowa Public Television. Email to confirm broadcast dates of Maintenance Shop Concert, May 27, 2016.

Zeitlin, Denny. Interview by author, May 13, 2019.

Interviews/Reports/Performances on Radio, Television, CDs

Bickal, Jim. *For Comedian Billy Crystal, All That (Dixieland) Jazz Is All in the Family*, Minnesota Public Radio, October 16, 2013, https://www.mprnews.org/story/2013/10/16/for-comedian-billy-crystal-all-that-dixieland-jazz-is-all-in-the-family.

Buckley, Dick. Bill Evans interview, WBEZ Radio, Chicago, August 1, 1979. Cassette courtesy of Joe La Barbera.

Borja, Svein Erik. Producer, NRK, *Bill Evans' Post-Concert Interview at the Molde, Norway Jazz Festival*, https://www.youtube.com/watch?v=UmvxPLFuHaM, (c. August 7, 1980).

Gair, Sondra. Interview with Bill Evans, WBEZ, November 14, 1976. Digital copy courtesy of Joe La Barbera.

Klabin, George. Interview with Bill Evans, *Pieces of Jade*, Resonance Records, 2009.

LaFaro, Scott. *My Foolish Heart*, Rehearsal Recording, *Pieces of Jade*, Resonance Records, 2009.

Merv Griffin Show. Bill Evans Performance on the Merv Griffin Show, August 23, 1980 (Taping), September 23, 1980 (Air date). Video courtesy of Joe La Barbera.

Norris, Michelle. *Billy Crystal: My Uncle Milt*, NPR, August 15, 2005, https://www.npr.org/templates/story/story.php?storyId=4601031.

O'Reilly, Ted. Interview with Bill Evans, Canadian Broadcasting Corporation, May 1980, Digital copy courtesy of Joe La Barbera.

Porter, Ross. Canadian Broadcasting Corporation, Radio Interview, *Bill Evans home and car interview by Ross Porter on JAZZFM91,* YouTube, https://www.youtube.com/watch?v=L1Sz5ZNokEA.

Rios, Simon. WBUR-FM, *Fred Taylor, Who Spent His Life Supporting the Boston Jazz Scene, Dies at 90*, October 26, 2019, https://www.wbur.org/artery/2019/10/26/fred-taylor-boston-jazz-scene.

Starns, Rod. Interview with Bill Evans, *Homecoming*, (Live concert CD), Milestone 1979.

Film and Video

Keane, Helen; Kenas, Peggy, Executive Producers, *The Universal Mind of Bill Evans: The Creative Process and Self Teaching*, https://www.youtube.com/watch?v=QwXAqIaUahI.

Spiegel, Bruce. Producer, Documentary Video, *Bill Evans Time Remembered*, 2015.

Website Links (Title)

'*58 Mile*s, Release date, 1974, https://en.wikipedia.org/wiki/1958_Miles, https://www.allmusic.com/album/58-sessions-featuring-stella-by-starlight-mw0000194393.

CBS 30th Street Studio, https://en.wikipedia.org/wiki/CBS_30th_Street_Studio.

Evans Discography, allmusic.com https://www.allmusic.com/artist/bill-evans-mn0000764702/discography.

Evans Grammy wins by 1979, https://www.grammy.com/grammys/artists/bill-evans/9689.

Jazz Track by Miles Davis, https://en.wikipedia.org/wiki/Jazz_Track; https://www.discogs.com/Miles-Davis-Jazz-Track/release/511939.

Laico, Frank. Engineering Credits, https://www.allmusic.com/artist/frank-laico-mn0000142372/credits.

Lenox History, February 11, 2016, https://lenoxhistory.org/lenoxhistorypeople andplaces/music-inn-lenox-school-jazz/.

L'Espace Cardin, History, Seating, https://fr.wikipedia.org/wiki/Espace_Cardin.

Live at the Village Vanguard titles, allmusic.com, https://www.allmusic.com/search/all/live%20at%20the%20village%20vanguard.

Manhattan Plaza, https://www.related.com/our-company/properties/manhattan-plaza; https://en.wikipedia.org/wiki/Manhattan_Plaza.

Mob ownership of The Sands, https://en.wikipedia.org/wiki/Sands_Hotel_and_Casino.

Maintenance Shop, Iowa State University, History, Club Size, https://www.discogs.com/label/1832695-The-Maintenance-Shop; https://www.sub.iastate.edu/maintenance-shop/history-of-the-venue/.

Rockefeller University, *The First Pharmacological Treatment for Narcotic Addiction: Methadone Maintenance*, http://centennial.rucares.org/index.php?page=Methadone_Maintenance.

Ronnie Scott's, History and acts, https://www.ronniescotts.co.uk/about-ronnies/club-history.

We Will Meet Again, Grammy Awards, https://www.grammy.com/grammys/awards/23rd-annual-grammy-awards-1980.

We Will Meet Again, allmusic.com rating, https://www.allmusic.com/album/we-will-meet-again-mw0000276230.

Website Links (Author)

Anderson, Faye. All That Philly Jazz, *Douglass Hotel*, April 7, 2015, https://phillyjazz.us/2015/04/07/douglass-hotel/.

Bickal, Jim. *For comedian Billy Crystal, all that (Dixieland) jazz is all in the family*, Minnesota Public Radio, October 16, 2013, https://www.mprnews.org/story/2013/10/16/for-comedian-billy-crystal-all-that-dixieland-jazz-is-all-in-the-family.

Borja, Svein Erik. Producer, NRK, *Bill Evans' Post-Concert Interview at the Molde, Norway Jazz Festival*, https://www.youtube.com/watch?v=UmvxPLFuHaM, (c. August 7, 1980).

Covert, James. *The Syms Saga: From Rags to Riches*, New York Post, November 3, 2011, https://nypost.com/2011/11/03/the-syms-saga-from-rags-to-riches-to-rags/.

Fricke, David. *Charlie Watts' Jazz Dream*, Rolling Stone, February 26, 1987, https://www.rollingstone.com/music/music-news/charlie-watts-jazz-dream-249051/.

Fried, Joseph. *Manhattan Plaza Wins Approval As Housing For Performing Artists*, New York Times, February 4, 1977, https://www.nytimes.com/1977/02/04/archives/manhattan-plaza-wins-approval-as-housing-for-performing-artists.html.

Hoffman, Steve. *History of CBS Records 30th Street Studio NYC*, https://forums.stevehoffman.tv/threads/history-of-cbs-records-30th-street-studio-nyc-many-pictures.388186/.

Keane, Helen; Kenas, Peggy, Executive Producers, *The Universal Mind of Bill Evans: The Creative Process and Self Teaching*, https://www.youtube.com/watch?v=QwXAqIaUahI.

Norris, Michelle, *Billy Crystal: My Uncle Milt*, NPR, August 15, 2005, https://www.npr.org/templates/story/story.php?storyId=4601031.

Porter, Ross. Canadian Broadcasting Corporation, Radio Interview, *Bill Evans home and car interview by Ross Porter on JAZZFM91*, YouTube, https://www.youtube.com/watch?v=L1Sz5ZNokEA.

Ben Ratliff, *Francis Paudras, 62, Patron of Jazz Pianist Bud Powell*, New York Times, December 17, 1997, https://www.nytimes.com/1997/12/17/arts/francis-paudras-62-patron-of-jazz-pianist-bud-powell.html.

Rios, Simon. WBUR-FM, *Fred Taylor, Who Spent His Life Supporting the Boston Jazz Scene, Dies at 90*, October 26, 2019, https://www.wbur.org/artery/2019/10/26/fred-taylor-boston-jazz-scene.

Stevens, Jan. Interview with Nenette Evans, The Bill Evans Webpages, https://www.billevanswebpages.com/nenette.html.

Teachout, Terry. *Suicide Was Painful*, New York Times, September 13, 1998, https://www.nytimes.com/1998/09/13/books/suicide-was-painful.html.

Shifrin, Carole. *Machinists Strike Against United Airlines*, Washington Post, March 31, 1979, https://www.washingtonpost.com/archive/politics/1979/03/31/machinists-strike-united-airlines/610c2eef-9f11-455d-912d-d3364d1ae08f/.

Watrous, Peter. *Max Gordon, 86, Jazz Promoter And Founder of Vanguard, Dies*, New York Times, May 12, 1989, https://www.nytimes.com/1989/05/12/obituaries/max-gordon-86-jazz-promoter-and-founder-of-vanguard-dies.html.

Weatherford, Mike. *Frank Sinatra*, Las Vegas Review Journal, February 7, 1999, https://www.reviewjournal.com/news/frank-sinatra/.

Williams, Martin. *The Jazz Hit of Montreux*, New York Times, January 5, 1969, https://www.nytimes.com/1969/01/05/archives/the-jazz-hit-of-montreux.html.

Yanow, Scott. *Turn Out The Stars,* Album review, allmusic.com, https://www.allmusic.com/album/turn-out-the-stars-final-village-vanguard-recordings-mw0000080506.

Index

C

D

F

Hughes, Mike, 16
Hunt, Joe, 85

I

"I Loves You, Porgy," 105
"If You Could See Me Now," 114
"In Your Own Sweet Way," 105, 140
International Association for Jazz Education, 158
Interplay, 17
Israels, Chuck, 17–18, 85, 166, 171–72

J

K

L

M

N

U 

Universal Mind of Bill Evans, The: The Creative Process and Self Teaching, 67, 93, 136
Urban, Georgia, 90–91

V

W 

X

Y

Z